THE FAMILY PARTY BOOK

CARYL KRUEGER

ABINGDON PRESS / Nashville

THE FAMILY PARTY BOOK

Copyright © 1996 by Caryl Krueger

This book is printed on recycled, acid-free paper.

Library of Congress Cataloging–in–Publication Data

Krueger, Caryl Waller, 1929–
    The family party book : 99 easy entertainment tips / Caryl Krueger.
        p.   cm.
    ISBN 0-687-01541-3 (pbk. : alk. paper)
    1. Entertaining—Planning. I. Title.
GV1471.K88   1996   96-19367
793.2—dc20   CIP

96 97 98 99 00 01 02 03 04 05 — 10 9 8 7 6 5 4 3 2 1

To

Claire, Max, and Cameron

and their parents

for all the exciting party times ahead

CONTENTS

ACKNOWLEDGMENTS 7

INTRODUCTION
Shall We Party? 9

CHAPTER 1
The Ten Rules for Entertaining with Ease 11

CHAPTER 2
Masterminding Your Party 13

CHAPTER 3
Gatherings for Grown-Ups 23

CHAPTER 4
Perfect Parties for Preschoolers 43

CHAPTER 5
Grade School Get-Togethers 59

CHAPTER 6
Teen Extravaganzas 77

CHAPTER 7
Holiday Celebrations 95

CHAPTER 8

Special Occasion? No Occasion? Party! 115

CHAPTER 9

Memorable Reunions Without Struggle 131

CHAPTER 10

99 Ideas for Successful Parties 149

THE PARTY-GIVER'S CREED 166

INDEX 167

ACKNOWLEDGMENTS

How could a party book be written successfully without help from our wonderful friends around the country! These good people have been guests at our home and have also kindly shared some of their own ideas for great celebrations:

Linda and Clarence Bargmann, Marylou Barrett, Linda Brown, Marianne Christian, Betty Copp, Evie Dorsher, Mary Ann Douglas, Jan Duke, Jennifer Dyck, Carol Fleisher, Evid Froehlich, Lynne Gerner, Lynn Grantham, Craig Hunter, Piper and Bruce Hunter, Jean and Jan Kater, Betty Kerr, Sheila Kinder, Connie King, Berit Kinter, Carrie Krueger, Diane and Cameron Krueger, Gladys Kuehl, Rudine Le Mons, Robin and Barry Long, Betty Lotz, Danielle McCune, Thelma MacGregor, Mary Miller, Dot Mitchell, Donna Montalbano, Dee Mossler, Jean Mosteller, Abby Nestvold, Elieth Robertshaw, Sue Sarture, Susan Shaw, Marge Schoeffel, Marjorie Sorensen, Betty Speicher, Norma Stirens, Jo Ann Tonet, Judy Trinkle, Lois Trunick, Edie Tower, Dr. Sandra Vavra, and Valerie Yancy.

INTRODUCTION

Shall We Party?

In today's fast-moving and sometimes fractured society, there are far too few occasions to have good times with good friends. People are working longer hours and having less time for leisure. And in many cases, television has taken over the free time that's left.

Still, some of the best memories of family life are times spent together with friends—from simple gatherings and surprise parties to festive feasts and heartwarming reunions. Adding entertaining to the family calendar can be tremendous fun, and as a bonus, it can also be educational. Spending time with friends or helping kids to entertain at home improves relationships, increases cooperation, and creates love within and beyond the family circle.

One reason that parties are often absent from family life is that we falsely believe that entertaining requires a lot of time, money, and energy—three things we may have in limited supply. But let me assure you that you can enjoy the company of friends several times a month and still keep yourself, your family, and your budget on an even keel. You just have to know how!

Parties are high on my list of family events. I love to plan them, prepare for them, and take part in them. And I'm even willing to clean up after them—although my husband usually takes on that challenge.

Because of our large, extended family, I've been responsible through the years for more than eighty kids' parties, thirty-five anniversary celebrations, forty Christmas parties, thirty-three office parties, thirty-five Thanksgiving reunions, and countless other celebrations for babies, dogs, ninety-year-olds, brides, and trade groups, as well as parties to welcome newcomers or say bon voyage to friends. I can easily cook party food for two best friends or for eighty of my husband's clients.

How to entertain—and most important, how to enjoy it—is the theme of this book. I'll help you go about it step-by-step so that you, too, will look forward with anticipation to your next celebration.

Caryl Krueger

1
The Ten Rules for Entertaining with Ease

Your first party shouldn't be to entertain the king and queen of Transylvania or forty athletic teenagers!

Hence, rule one: Start with a small intimate affair.

One to four guests is ideal. Even if you're not a complete novice, you may want to work up from small and simple to large and elegant.

Rule two: Let the food be secondary.

Unless gourmet cooking is your passion, keep the food simple—meaning easy-to-prepare and not expensive. And by doing so, you'll have a better chance of not overwhelming your guests—thus, they'll feel comfortable about "having you back."

Rule three: Don't be the Little Red Hen and try to do it all yourself.

Learn to graciously accept the help of friends in various aspects of a party. And when the party is to involve children—whether they are toddlers or teens—involve the youngsters in the planning, execution, and follow-up. Sometimes this can be as much fun as the party itself.

Rule four: Plan ahead and have free time on the party date.

In order to enjoy the party, you shouldn't be burdened with other major concerns. Choose a time when everyone is feeling well, there are no major household

renovations going on, and there are no anticipated crises or deadlines at your job. Although you can do most of the planning and many of the foods ahead, have some extra time on the party date for the unexpected—which usually happens!

Rule five: Entertain just for the fun of it.

Don't wait for something momentous to celebrate. Certainly you'll have a golden wedding anniversary party, but plan lots of other parties in the years beforehand!

Rule six: Schedule tentative party plans for the months ahead.

Look at your calendar in three-month chunks. See what birthdays and anniversaries will require parties and must be woven into your entertainment plan. Then add some "just because" parties as described in chapter 8. Over a three-month period, try to host four or five events—some small, some larger gatherings.

Rule seven: Entertain the day after the house is cleaned.

Although a clean house doth not a party make, you certainly don't want to be cited by the sanitation department. But unless you have the kind of friends who check out the closets and cupboards, you only need to be sure that the entertainment room, kitchen, and one bathroom are presentable—work easily done the day before your party.

Rule eight: Be sure to entertain those who entertain you.

Many people love to go to parties but never entertain in return. Cross these sponges off your entertaining list! Don't make excuses for them such as "they have a small apartment" or "they're so busy." If they really wanted to be your friends, they could at least order in a pizza to share with you.

Rule nine: Create a file folder called "Entertaining" and keep it up-to-date.

Establish a record of who was invited and who actually attended, what you did, what you ate. I learned this when one kind guest said, "Oh, I just love the way you always make blue cheese hamburgers." Unfortunately, I had no recollection of what I'd served them previously. So I resolved right then to keep a brief description of each party.

Rule ten: Read this book and open an exciting new chapter in your life.

It's just fine to spend an evening with friends chatting and eating popcorn. But it's also pleasant to entertain with some style. You can do this with ease if you pay special attention to the next chapter of this book: "Masterminding Your Party." In it, I'll take you moment-by-moment through the preparation stage and right up to the time you close the door behind the happy, departing guests.

2
Masterminding Your Party

It's five minutes before your party is to start. Are you still-in-the-kitchen-looking-for-the-napkins-and-trying-to-keep-two-pots-from-boiling-over-while-engaging-in-a-shouting-match-with-your-daughter-who-won't-put-on-her-PJs-and-at-the-same-time-doing-long-range-consulting-with-your-husband-about-what-shirt-looks-best-with-his-new-slacks? Or are you sitting serenely in the living room thumbing through a magazine?

At our house, we treasure the fifteen minutes before the guests arrive. It's a quiet time to admire the sparkling house, to talk with each other about the good people coming, and to think through what each of us will do in the next few hours. There's no match for this golden-glow time before the event! And when you mastermind your party correctly, you'll have this essential relaxation time.

In masterminding your party, you need to know in advance how much help you are going to have. Will your spouse pitch in before the party, during the party, and afterward? Entertaining is neither masculine nor feminine, and parties are best when both spouses are involved.

What about your children? Would they be interested in helping with advance preparations? Can one serve the appetizer? Clear the table? Clean up the kitchen? You may want to offer a "butler's fee" for this kind of extra service. Our own grown children are avid entertainers because they were involved in party preparations since early childhood. So don't wait 'til the kids leave home to have parties!

In many decades of entertaining, I've only had a catered party twice. But I have had competent help from family and friends. Perhaps you have a child, grandchild, or young neighborhood friend who'd like to earn extra money by helping. Especially for a large event, this added help makes it run more smoothly and leaves you calm and better able to enjoy your own party.

If you are entertaining alone, you need organization all the more. Perhaps one of the guests will offer to make part of the meal such as the salad, or help you by clearing dishes or serving the coffee. If you can't count on this kind of help, you may need to simplify your plans, but it's still important to entertain (that way you get entertained in return). Your entertaining may be done in conjunction with going to a movie and returning home for cake, or providing a picnic for a sporting event. Or, you can have an elaborate dinner party all done with your own two hands because you know how to mastermind the event.

EVERY PARTY NEEDS A MASTER PLAN

Whether your party is going to be a team effort or a solo endeavor, you need a master plan. For many decades, I've organized my parties this way, and for your own peace of mind and a memorable party, I heartily recommend this method.

While this plan is for an adult party, you can easily adapt it for a child's or teen's party. The same preparation is usually needed, except you'll have the kids to help you.

KEEPING A RECORD

Will you always remember who attended, who regretted, and what was served? Why wonder when you can *know* by keeping a simple record? Whether you do it by hand or in the computer, do it! Keep these lists in your "Entertaining" file for later reference. The form on the next page is one I like.

CHOOSING THE DATE AND TIME

Well in advance, consult your calendar and pick a date that is relatively free of other activities. Parties have no season, so plan them for all kinds of weather. (One host had a party in the summer and told guests to "Wear as little as the censors will allow." The resulting garb was humorous but very comfortable!)

Choose a time that will not pressure those who work away from home (including yourself). Allow guests time to return from work, change into party attire, and arrive on time. Select a memorable time such as 6:10 or 7:15. This calls more attention to the time, and thus guests are more apt to arrive right on schedule.

SELECTING THE THEME

Decide if this is going to be a patio picnic, an evening of desserts and charades, or a teen DJ party. In the invitation, let guests know the general theme so they'll know how to dress.

The following chapters of this book give you a variety of tested ideas, but you can certainly come up with your own good themes. Be sure that you're selecting a theme that you will enjoy executing, and also one that you can afford. A too elaborate theme can be costly, and thus when the bills come in you may remember the price more than the party.

Some themes are worth repeating. One host gives an annual Academy Awards party, another a yearly Independence Day barbecue.

DATE: (Day of week, date, month, year) _____

PLACE: (If not at home) _____

THEME: _____

GUEST LIST: Accepted   Regretted

_____

_____

_____

_____

_____

_____

INVITATION: (Attach sample if written rather than phoned)

DRESS: _____

ACTIVITIES: _____

  Preparation time:

  Cost of favors/prizes:

FOOD SERVED: _____

_____

  Preparation time:

  Approximate cost:

  Table linens used:

WHAT MIGHT HAVE BEEN DONE DIFFERENTLY: _____

_____

COMMENTS: (Your own, or from guests) _____

_____

EXTENDING THE INVITATION

For casual get-togethers, a few phone calls can take care of the inviting process. For larger parties, you will want to send a written invitation. This is helpful and timesaving since the exact date, time, theme, and apparel are all spelled out.

Important! Be sure to put in an RSVP line—and underline it! After the letters RSVP (the French abbreviation for *repondez s'il vous plaît* meaning "reply if you please"), put the word *by* followed by the date that is a week before your party. You are entitled to know that far in advance who is coming.

Unfortunately, some people are quite sloppy about letting you know if they plan to attend. There are those who assume you're a mind reader and should just know that they'll be there, or that they'll be out of town. Then there's the category of invitees who appear to be waiting to RSVP until they see what their options are—if they'll somehow get a better invitation. If guests treat you this way, cross them off your list forever.

Some socially uncouth folks may have to be telephoned on the day after the one listed for your RSVP. Don't take *maybe* for an answer unless someone isn't feeling well, but hopes to recover. Just state simply that you have to plan ahead, so you need to know. Don't be apologetic—they should be apologizing to *you* for failing to RSVP. A week ahead you should know the exact number of guests.

If it's a huge bash and you don't need to know the specific names, you can write "Regrets only" on the invitation, but this can be dangerous since some people neither regret nor come. Better to be specific and give a date for responses.

Along with the pertinent information on your invitation, you may want to enclose a map if your location isn't easy to find.

PLANNING THE ACTIVITIES

Much party planning can be done "in the cracks"—in those moments when you're alone in the car, folding laundry, brushing your teeth, polishing shoes. Use these minutes as think times to get in mind what activities you'd like to include. You can also have a family brainstorming session to come up with more good ideas. If it's a child's party, it's extremely important to include his/her ideas on activities and refreshments.

Make a list of what activities are involved: A cocktail time? Treasure hunt? Sit-down dinner? Relay race? Songfest? Choose activities that fit your guests, your theme, your budget, and your time.

PLANNING THE FOOD

Once you know your theme and activities, decide how important food will be—a meal, dessert, or snacks. Remember that nowadays most people eat smaller portions, eat healthier, and eat more leisurely. So unless you really want leftovers, don't plan on lots of extra food. (An exception to this is a teen party where they inhale huge quantities of seminutritious foods preceded and followed by chips and sodas!)

Unless you're making a soufflé (usually a dangerous idea) or doing last-minute stir-fry cooking, you can prepare many of your foods in advance. There are wonderful recipes that *must* be made the day before or eight hours before serving. Go for those if you don't enjoy the last-minute stress and mess.

Make a list of everything you plan to serve, from appetizers to after-dinner mints. This will help you prepare your grocery shopping list.

THE COUNTDOWN FOR THE WEEK AHEAD

It can be an exhilarating test of your skills to do all the preparations for a party on the very day of the event. But I don't like last-minute panic, so I work ahead, doing certain tasks ahead of time. Buy many of the foods the week before and only the fresh items forty-eight hours ahead. Put a dessert and homemade bread or rolls in the freezer, make the salad dressing.

One time I had to return from out of town on the evening before I hosted a large luncheon. This meant that almost everything was done in advance. Yes, there are cakes that love to be frozen, casseroles that can be thawed the morning of an event, even fruit salads that you can take from your freezer and get rave notices for. This luncheon again proved the merit of advance food preparations.

In the week before your party, get the activities completely ready to go. If decorations are involved, prepare those, too. Purchase and wrap any gifts or prizes. Make place cards and figure out the seating arrangement.

Clean the house and sweep sidewalks and porches the day before the party. Set out guest towels and soap, explaining to kids that these are for company only. Of course there will be some places you'll have to check out on party day, but do the major work ahead of time. This is where you can definitely get help from the family.

Pick out what you plan to wear. If other family members will be at the party, have them do the same. You don't need any last minute surprises with missing buttons or uncoordinated jewelry or unironed shirts.

Set the buffet and tables a day or two before. Bring out your cooking pans, serving dishes, trivets, and utensils. You'll be amazed at how much can be accomplished beforehand!

THE COUNTDOWN ON THE DAY OF THE PARTY

How astute you feel when you are in control and have everything done ahead of time! Here's a sample countdown for the day of the party—a buffet supper called for six o'clock. (The menu is meat loaf, make-ahead mashed potatoes, fresh asparagus with crumb topping, tropical fruit salad, lemon cake. Two appetizers and drinks are served before dinner, candy afterwards.) The two appetizers, meat loaf, mashed potatoes, asparagus topping, and cake should be in the freezer from an earlier kitchen session. (If you don't have the wonderful recipe for make-ahead mashed potatoes, it's given in chapter 10, #35.)

Morning:

1. Cut flowers and put in deep water. (Some floral arrangements can be made the day before.)
2. Prepare asparagus (or any other food that was not done earlier in the week).
3. Prepare fruit salad. (Dressing was made earlier in week.)
4. Take all foods that need to be thawed out from the freezer (potatoes, cake, appetizers)
5. Put filled water pitcher in the refrigerator and ice cubes in bowl or ice bucket in the freezer. Cut lemon wedges for water glasses and refrigerate.
6. Wash up all dishes and wipe counters.
7. See that materials for activities are in place.
8. Arrange flowers.
9. Prepare candy dishes.

Afternoon:

1. Tidy the house, especially entry, living room, family room, bathroom. (You've cleaned the day before.)
2. Empty the dishwasher.
3. Give kitchen final cleanup after lunch.
4. Set up coffee service, including sugar and cream.
5. Arrange area where appetizers and beverages are to be served.
6. Enjoy a nonparty activity with family, or read and rest.

Final time schedule:

4:30—Put main dish in oven. (This is the time needed for a large meat loaf that bakes 1½ hours and then must sit before slicing. Adjust this time for your own main dish.) Set timer for when it should come out and note this on your time schedule.

4:35—Dress, and put on apron (yes, male chefs, too).

5:00—Put potatoes in oven. Note when they should come out.
Lay out salad plates.
Cook asparagus to minus five minutes.
Put lemon wedges in water glasses.

5:15—Put appetizers (made day before or earlier) on serving plates in refrigerator.
Turn on coffee.
Check status of main dish, potatoes, vegetable. Sometimes you may want to use a warming tray, but it's better to have them come out of the oven at the right time.
Put salad in serving bowl or on individual plates.

5:35—Put plenty of ice cubes in glasses.
Check on main dish, potatoes, vegetable.

Bring predinner beverages to where they'll be served.
Turn on background music and lights on as needed.
5:45—Sit down!
5:55—Bring appetizers to where they'll be served.
6:00—Guests arrive! The fun begins.
6:30—Set out buffet foods (plates are already on buffet).
Fill water glasses.
Light candles.
Check that all burners/ovens/warmers are off.

This type of planning leaves nothing to a faulty memory, and lets you confidently and graciously spend time with family and friends. I suggest you write out a chart like this for both the advance preparations and the day of each party. Make it your practice to work this way, saving yourself time, worry, and potential embarrassment.

ENORMOUS PARTIES

I used exactly the same type of scheduling when hosting an office party for eighty-five guests. However, I planned a turkey almondine casserole that I could prepare a few weeks before (actually I made and froze ten of them to feed eighty-five and have some second helpings). With it I served a cabbage salad that must be made the day before. I put this in large airtight plastic bags in the refrigerator. The made-ahead dressing was added just before serving. The appetizers (a hot crab dip, three kinds of tortilla roll-ups, and chili cheese quiche) were made the day before.

When I took the ten casseroles out to thaw the day before the party, I put eight ice-cream desserts into the freezer—a dessert that was to be served directly from the freezer. The only cooking I did on the party day was preparing the loaves of bread with garlic/cheese butter wrapped in foil for heating. With this menu, I served a big bowl of spiced red crab apples—a colorful, slightly sweet touch—the kind you can buy ready to serve.

Advance plans included many things related to a large party:

1. Writing a good invitation requesting an RSVP so we could plan ahead.
2. Accumulating dinner and dessert forks, china dinner plates (a dear neighbor helped), buying the best quality plastic glasses and cups, as well as large colorful paper napkins.
3. Borrowing a large coffeemaker, rectangular casserole dishes, card tables, chairs, and some tablecloths, also hot trays for keeping casseroles hot after baking.
4. Preparing (a day ahead) table centerpieces with flowers and candles.
5. Asking a friend to check bathrooms for towels and tissue halfway through the party.
6. Reconfirming arrival time of the entertainment—a hot air balloon tethered behind our house! Everyone was thrilled to ride up in the air one-hundred feet to see the views.
7. Planning for parking. Alerting neighbors as a courtesy—many offered their own driveways.
8. Locating rubbish cans, sparking clean and with liners, on decks and patios.
9. Putting a small note on each table asking one person only to bring dinner plates to the kitchen and return with dessert.

10. Hiring a helper to tidy up after the appetizer time, help with the buffet and dessert, and then wash all the dishes and clean up the kitchen.
11. Arranging for a good photographer friend to take pictures of the event.
12. Being ready early so as to greet everyone at the front gate and having a friend at a nearby table with prelettered name tags.
13. Asking one person to direct guests at dinner time to the many tables, and see that each table was filled.
14. Asking a few willing men to fold up tables and chairs at the end of the party.

Yes, it was a great event! We immediately started planning the topper!

TRIALS AND TRIBULATIONS

Sometimes things don't turn out as planned. A special guest suddenly can't come. The roof leaks in the living room. That good cut of meat is incredibly tough. A game bombs. So what? Unexpected things just happen and are no reflection on you as a party-giver. Don't give them a second thought. A little self-deprecating humor and a big smile will put you and your guests at ease.

Some of the best parties include spontaneity. For one special party I'd worked hard preparing and then initiating a game that night. Suddenly—right in the middle of the game—we heard sirens in the distance. Our twelve guests rushed out onto the deck where, across a little valley, we could see a large abandoned house fully engulfed in flames. Knowing that no one was in danger, we watched the outline of the blaze against the night sky. And, we learned a lot about knocking down a fire when all the sophisticated equipment arrived. In the notes and calls that followed that party, no one commented on my clever games or tasty food, but they were impressed at the lengths we'd go to in order to provide exciting entertainment!

Often you'll learn from a mistake. After dinner at a party we were giving, I went to retrieve from the oven a wonderful warm chocolate soufflé. I had planned on making a grand entrance with this high, puffy delicacy (which bakes in the forty minutes during dinner). However, I was deflated to see that it too looked deflated, in fact it was just as I had last seen it—like chocolate soup. Well, it seemed that a well-meaning spouse had noted just before dinner that the oven was on, and helpfully turned it off!

Since murder wasn't an option, we laughingly told the guests what had happened and said it was up to them to entertain us with witty conversation for the next forty minutes. They all rose to the occasion, and the around-the-table chatting time was both delightful and stimulating. Three-quarters of an hour passed quickly and the great chocolate soufflé was served with a flourish—and applause.

WHAT HAPPENS AFTER . . .

Of course, there's party cleanup to do when the last guest has gone home. But that's a good opportunity for an assessment of the party while it's still fresh in mind.

Consider these points:

* Was the mix of guests good—people of varied backgrounds and interests?
* Was the time allotted for conversation, eating, and activities sufficient and not rushed?
* What activities were most successful?
* What was the highlight of the party?
* What foods could be repeated another time?
* Considering the effort put in, was it worth it?

Don't forget to write your opinions on your party record form.

BE AN ENTERTAINER

Don't fall into the leech or sponge category. When you're invited to a gathering, do your best to respond in kind by inviting your hosts to one of your parties. (Good manners prescribe no more than a six-month wait between being entertained and entertaining in return.)

Of course, if it turns out that you don't enjoy the folks who entertained you, you don't have to entertain back, but remember, you should not accept another invitation from them—that's being a leech. And certainly avoid being a sponge—copying someone else's menu and activities!

Try the ideas in this book and develop your own good style. Don't be a host who always entertains with beer and TV sports. Be willing to try new things. Great party-givers have many little gimmicks they use to make parties go smoothly, so you'll want to benefit from their helpful tidbits in the last chapter of this book. But between this chapter and the last, you'll find ideas for ninety-nine grand parties.

3
Gatherings for Grown-Ups

When you get together with friends—old or new—your event usually falls into one of two categories: the party has a theme, or it's just a casual occasion to eat and talk. Both kinds of parties can be enjoyable. The right mix of friends sitting around the fire with mugs of soup can bring about spirited conversation and camaraderie. Almost everyone knows how to give this kind of party.

But it's also fun to have a well-planned party—to create the theme, then select the people, the food, the decor, the activities, and games. This style of entertaining you'll do less often, but if it's done right, it will be a memorable event. Here are some *Do's* and *Don'ts* to help your adult party go smoothly:

- Decide first on the theme. Don't make it too elaborate or expensive—after all, you don't want to intimidate your friends and you *do* want to be invited to their parties.
- Choose the guests carefully. Along with the gregarious extroverts, include some introspective types. Mix in new acquaintances with old pals.
- Unless you can afford the luxury of a caterer, select a menu that allows you to make almost all foods in the days before the party, a few to prepare on party day, and nothing that will keep you kitchen-bound and away from your guests for more than fifteen minutes.
- Focus (rather than sprinkle around) your decor. If you are having a western barbecue, put a sawhorse with borrowed saddle at the front door. Arrange wild flowers in an old cowboy hat for the table centerpiece, use a horseshoe to keep the napkins from littering the yard, and ring an old-fashioned dinner bell to let folks know that the food is ready. That's all the decor you need. Forget the balloons and streamers!

- Don't overplan the activities and games. Usually you don't need to provide entertainment with the appetizers—people are happy to talk when they first meet. Save your clever ideas for dinnertime and later. Don't have activities that are all athletic or all intellectual. (One paper and pencil game per party is enough!)

If you're a novice party-giver, be sure to read chapters 1 and 2 for further ideas on organizing a successful party.

FIVE TOP-RATED PARTIES

These winning events are all quite different and run the range from athletic to aesthetic, from casual to costumed. They are appealing to a wide variety of ages and interests.

1. The Time Capsule Party

GUESTS: This party works best for twelve to fifty of your friends, and it isn't necessary that they all know one another, as the party provides opportunities for invitees to get acquainted.

THEME: The idea of actually burying a time capsule is intriguing, especially if guests know they will be invited back years later to dig it up! This is an ideal party for a house under construction, but there's no reason you can't do it at another time. (The couple who held this party when their house was being built entertained on the patio where guests sat at brightly covered tables centered with colorful potted daisies they'd planned to plant in their garden after the party.)

LENGTH OF PARTY: This depends on the number of guests invited. Average time will be three to four hours.

INVITATION: Written invitations are needed in order to give all the facts. Guests are asked to bring a small object of their choice to be buried in a time capsule. They are told that they will explain to the others the significance of their item. The invitation should also invite them back for the party to unearth the capsule—in year 2005 or whatever year you've selected.

DECOR: None needed, just festive tables for dining and chairs for sitting. For a hot day, umbrellas (or a shady patio) are recommended.

ACTIVITIES/GAMES: The magic of this party begins when the first guest starts telling about his or her donation to the capsule. If guests don't know one another, the host should first tell how each friendship began, relating a warm or funny anecdote. Then the person rises, shows, and tells about the contribution. Some will make predictions, too, and these add to the fun. You may want to make a recording of these little talks to replay at the later party. Each donation is labeled with the person's name.

When all the items are described, make a ceremony of packing them into a waterproof container and burying them, each person taking a turn with the shovel. Mark the spot with a boulder so you can find it again and so you won't pour a concrete patio slab over it by mistake. The important aspect of this party is that it gives each person a platform for expressing individuality. It's also a great record of your friendships.

FOOD: Depending on the time for the party, you can have snacks or a meal. At one time capsule party, guests were asked to bring a food they thought they might be eating in the year 2010. These "foods of the future" included custard (the ideal food for old folks), dishes made of tofu and soybeans, energy bars, nonfat yogurt dips, and fat-free desserts.

PRIZES/FAVORS: None needed.

PLANNING AHEAD: Other than the refreshments, you'll want to dig a hole for the time capsule and obtain a large waterproof and sealable container.

2. The Pentathlon Party

GUESTS: Although this sounds like a party for jocks, sports ability doesn't count much. It works well with teens, singles, seniors, and even couch potatoes. About twelve to twenty guests are ideal.

THEME: It's based on five events, and you can tailor these to your guests. Choose your five games from this list: golf ball putting, darts, Velcro ball toss, relay races, table tennis, pick-up-sticks or a Jenga game, chess or checkers, Monopoly, Trivial Pursuit, or another board or card game.

INVITATIONS: Send invitations decorated with advertising pictures of athletic shoes or equipment. Suggest sports clothes as the attire. Don't give more details.

DECOR: Nothing needed.

LENGTH OF PARTY: Three hours or more. The games will take about two hours, plus an initial time to explain the pentathlon and the rotation, and time for dessert and awards at the end.

ACTIVITIES/GAMES: Games are set up in advance in different areas such as living room, family room, hallway, patio, lawn, and so forth. Participants play each game for just twenty minutes, then rotate to another, eventually playing all five games. Guests not playing can be referees or observers. Several timers are set to indicate the eighteen-minute point as a two-minute warning.

In advance, prepare a very large scoreboard with games listed horizontally across the top and with a final column for total points. Put players' names down the left side. Input individual scores after each round.

Here are the details of some games you can play. Choose five.

1. Putting. You'll need a golf ball, putter, and bright thread. In the middle of a carpeted room, make a six-inch diameter circle of thread. Also make a starting line about eight feet away. Each player gets five chances to one-putt the ball into the thread circle. Scoring: five points for each ball in the circle, three points for each ball touching the circle. If no ball gets into or touches the circle, the ball nearest the circle gets two points.

2. Darts. In an area without foot traffic, put up a dartboard and protect the surrounding wall as necessary. Each player gets five chances to hit the bull's-eye. Scoring: five points for a bull's-eye, four, three, two, or one point for farther out hits on the dartboard.

3. *Ball toss.* You'll need a stopwatch, two Velcro mitts and ball (an inexpensive purchase at a toy store if you don't have a set). In a hallway or outside level area, use string or chalk to mark two lines twenty feet apart. Each player gets a partner and a few practice tosses. The partners, standing behind opposite lines, will toss the ball back and forth. An observer with stopwatch will count the number of catches (no bounces) in a three-minute period. This is the score for both partners. For a small party, you can let players choose a second partner and try for a better score.

4. *Pick-up-sticks or Jenga.* Two opponents play the game according to the game rules. The winner gets ten points.

5. *Chess or checkers.* Two opponents play the game, the winner gets ten points.

6. *Monopoly.* Two to four can play at once. In advance, put houses and hotels on properties and divide the money equally. Shuffle and deal the property cards to the players. Otherwise, follow the regular rules. After eighteen minutes, players count their money and reset the board for the next group. The one with the most money gets ten points, second place gets five points, then three or one point for the two players with the least cash.

7. *Trivial Pursuit and other board games.* You can adapt trivia games, dominoes, Tripoly, and other board games to make a total of five games for your Pentathlon.

FOOD: Let players eat as they play. At each of the five game locations serve snacks usually associated with sports: peanuts, popcorn, Cracker Jack, trail mix, or nachos. In a central location, provide a variety of sports drinks (like Gatorade) plus hot dogs and fixings. When everyone has finished the five games, serve dessert and let the scorekeeping host announce the winners.

PRIZES: Applause is sufficient, but if you want to give prizes, tie in to the sporty theme. Some suggestions: tennis or golf balls, a sports towel, soap-on-a-rope, a headband or visor, sunscreen, trail mix or granola bars. One group that has a yearly Pentathlon Party with the same guests bought an inexpensive trophy that rotates to the winners' homes.

PLANNING AHEAD: The food for this party is easy, but you'll need to spend time setting up your games and the scoreboard.

3. *The Tempura Party*

While the previous two parties have focused on activities and games, the highlight of this party is definitely the Japanese food. (Tempura is vegetables and fish that are dipped in a batter, then deep-fried. Tempura mix is readily available at the market if you don't want to make your own. If you've never made it, I would advise you to practice in advance.)

GUESTS: Invite two to six friends, depending on the size of your eating area, since it's better to have everyone close together and able to reach the cooking pot.

THEME: Japanese tempura cooking, along with Japanese art and literature. Don't confuse Asian cooking styles—this is not an occasion for Chinese fortune cookies!

LENGTH OF PARTY: Two hours or more, depending on how much you eat and how long you talk!

INVITATION: Telephoned invitations are fine, or send the details of the party tucked into origami (Japanese folded paper art that's easy and fun to do).

DECOR: A low table and cushion seating is a lovely touch, but the regular dining room table works just as efficiently and, for Westerners, this may be more comfortable. Cover the table with newspaper, then with a plastic cloth or one that washes easily, since there may be some spills from pot to plate.

ACTIVITIES/GAMES: The action here is the food! The guests will be cooking their own dinner, bit by bit. Borrow Japanese picture books from the library, also a book of haiku poetry to be read while cooking progresses, and a book explaining origami paper folding.

FOOD: Almost all of the ingredients are prepared in advance, but cooked at the table. You will want trays of fish such as shrimps or scallops, and vegetables, such as peppers (red, green, and yellow), sweet potatoes or yams, watercress, broccoli, carrots, and pea pods. Cut ingredients into bite-size pieces and arrange attractively on one or two platters since color and visual presentation are very important to a Japanese meal. Serve individual bowls of cooked rice. Provide soy sauce and fish sauce. A simple dessert can be chilled fruits such as lichees (fresh or canned), orange segments, or pears, served with ginger cookies. Be prepared to make the tempura batter during the party—yes, you can do it at the table, following the simple package instructions.

Guests gather around the table, each person within reach of the special tempura cooker (or a pot of oil on a burner). The bowls of rice and tempura, and trays of foods are on the table. Provide chopsticks (learning to use them is fun) and longer cooking chopsticks or tongs for placing items in the hot oil. An item is ready when it appears crispy and slightly brown.

Take turns reading haiku, doing origami, looking at pictures from Japan, and talking about Japan. With the cooking going on constantly—and people sharing which are their favorites—there will be no shortage of conversation.

PLANNING AHEAD: Get reading material from the library. Buy colored paper for origami. On the day of the party you can easily prepare all of the food and set the table. You will make the tempura batter as you go along. Use Japanese paper napkins if you can find them at an Asian market.

4. "I'm a Song" Dinner Party

Although no musical ability is required to have lots of fun at this party, it does help if some of the group enjoy gathering around the piano for singing.

GUESTS: This party works best with twelve to twenty-four invitees—of all ages.

THEME: Music of all varieties, funny costumes, musical foods (explained later).

INVITATION: Cut sheet music into nine-by-four-inch rectangles that will fit into business-size envelopes. Write the details of the party on colored paper and paste in the center of the piece of sheet music. Include the request that each guest come dressed as a song, keeping the song name a secret.

LENGTH OF PARTY: Don't rush this fun event. The minimum time will be about four hours from "Hello Dolly" to "Goodnight, Ladies."

DECOR: While a piano is nice, one isn't necessary. Place simple musical instruments around the party area where guests can easily find them and try them (castanets, bongo drums, kazoo, harmonica, cymbals, keyboard, triangle, guitar, tambourine). The costumed guests will be adequate scenery.

ACTIVITIES/GAMES:

1. *"What Song Am I?"* As guests arrive, remind them not to tell what song they represent, but rather to let others guess. Provide plenty of appetizers in various locations so guests move about, looking at all the costumes. Have a ballot box so everyone can vote for his favorite costumed person. Guessing what song each guest represents will be the main source of fun. Some easy-to-costume songs include: "Three Blind Mice," "I'm Dreaming of a White Christmas," "You Ain't Nothing but a Hound Dog," "Phantom of the Opera," and "I've Been Working on the Railroad."

2. *Song Notes.* When it's time for dinner, hand each woman (or half of the guests) a slip of paper with the name of a song, and each man (or the other guests) the name of a musical (from which the songs were taken). Let them find each other and then sit together for dinner.

3. *Song Stumpers.* During dinner, encourage the guests to call out song titles and see who can be the first to sing it. You'll hear some unique titles and some interesting singing!

4. *Name That Tune.* After dinner divide the group into two teams and play a very short phrase of a song on the piano, or from a cassette. The team with the most correct guesses wins. Or you can play charades, acting out well-known songs.

If the group has some musical members, encourage group or individual singing. If not, buy a quantity of kazoos and have a kazoo marching band—this can be hilarious. Near the end of the party, give the prize for the best costume or costumes.

FOOD: Provide plenty of appetizers. For dinner, tie the foods in with songs: fillet of sole ("O Sole Mio"), tomato aspic ("You Say Tomato, I Say Tomato"), rice (the Wedding March), cake ("Happy Birthday to You"). You can get as cute as you want here or just sing "Amoré" and serve pizza!

PRIZES: For after-dinner game winners, applause will be sufficient. Provide a nice prize for the best costume, perhaps a cassette of a current musical or favorite group.

PLANNING AHEAD: Organize your food in advance so you still have plenty of energy to enjoy this fun party. Plan your own costume. Pick out recorded background music to use during the early part of the party. Gather the little instruments, make ballots and ballot box, get paper and pencils ready for games. Make a list of songs for "Name That Tune." Get out sheet music to encourage group singing.

5. The South Seas Islands Party

Everyone loves the lazy lure of island life. Although this sounds like a summer party, it can be a welcome change to the cold winter's social scene.

GUESTS: Invite twelve to twenty-four friends, depending on the size of your entertaining area. It's fine if this party is crowded.

THEME: Islandmania with flowers, palms, hula girls, and ukuleles—all things that tie in with Polynesia.

LENGTH OF PARTY: Three to four hours, or longer if you decide to show a film (see below).

INVITATION: Write your invitation on colored paper and place in a small, sealable plastic bag that you've filled with sand. Put the bag in an envelope and mail. Tell guests to dress for a trip to the south sea islands. (This lets some wear comfortable cruise-type clothes, while others go overboard with grass skirts or sarongs.)

DECOR: Keep the lights low and have romantic island music in the background. Present flowers or paper leis at the door. (A single flower worn over the right ear means "available," over the left ear means "taken," and in the middle of the head it indicates "undecided.") In one corner of the party area make an "island" by heaping many blankets and pillows, and then covering them with beach towels. Add other decor to the island such as a fake palm or other tree, shells, a cardboard tiki, a treasure chest filled with snacks, or hang paper fish from the ceiling. Take a Polaroid picture of each guest on this island.

ACTIVITIES/GAMES: People-watching will take much of the time before dinner. Afterward, here are some activities:

1. *Stranded!* With the group sitting in a circle in the same room with the island, start the sentence, "I was stranded on an island and was glad I had along . . ." The first person names something that begins with the letter A (an aardvark, an Apple computer, an atlas). The next person repeats the sentence and the A item and adds his own B item. So it goes around the circle. Those who forget or get stuck, must go and sit on the desert island. (It's fun when nearly everyone is crowded on the island.)

2. *Island Mysteries.* Blindfold one person and hand her an item she might use on a South Seas island. Have her describe it and how she'd use it. Make your items unusual such as a

roll of film, a tube of glue, a balloon, a rock, a small plastic bag of rice, a toothpick, a wooden spoon, a breath mint.

3. *Video Time.* Rent an old-time classic South Seas Islands video—choose from the Hope and Crosby "Road to . . ." films or the Jon Hall/Dorothy Lamour movie *Hurricane.* You may want to show the first twenty minutes of the film before dinner while you put the finishing touches on the food. After eating and playing games, you can show the remainder of the film if you wish.

FOOD: It has to be a luau, but you don't need a whole pig unless you want to make an *imu* (oven) in your backyard. Serve roast pork or mahimahi fillets, poi (available at the market), fruit salad, sweet potatoes, banana bread, and volcano cake (recipe at the end of this chapter). For appetizers, serve shrimp, curried cheese, or the appetizer given at the end of this chapter. Guava/passion fruit juice is a great drink.

PRIZES: Two for best costume winners. You may also want to give a special award to "the person I'd most like to be stranded on an island with."

PLANNING AHEAD: Using the organizational chart in chapter 2, make the cake and banana bread days or weeks ahead and freeze them. Build your island, rent the film, have a Polaroid camera, buy prizes, and gather the items for game #2. And of course, plan your own costume.

MORE PARTY THEMES

1. *Heavenly Parties.* meteors, eclipses, and space shots. Who says parties have to end by 11:00 P.M.? A unique party can be built around the action in the heavens. Each year there are nights with meteor showers or visible comets. Plan a late night party for one of these occasions with dinner at eight and then a little education (available in the newspaper or encyclopedia) followed by actually viewing the event. Provide lawn chairs and outdoor reclining chairs, sleeping bags and blankets.

    One of the best parties we ever gave was when the astronauts first walked on the moon. We lived in Hawaii where it was night when the walk took place. Ten families were invited to camp on our lawn. With a clear view of the moon, a few telescopes, and several television sets at the edge of the lawn, we all watched the landing and thrilled to the activities thereafter. The exciting part was that at the same time we saw on TV astronauts walking on the moon, we were also looking at the moon itself! By around two in the morning almost everyone had fallen asleep. My husband and I got up at 6:30 A.M. to make vast quantities of pancakes, which were served before everyone went on their way filled with unforgettable memories.

2. *The Investment Club Party.* Many men and women take a very personal interest in their finances and needs for the future. Invite about twenty friends to hear a talk on investments (local speakers from investment firms will usually come free) and enjoy snacks and conversation. Then decide if you want to have a monthly gathering, pool funds, and actually make investments. One such successful club even has a Christmas party where each participant brings a gift purchased from one of the companies they have shares in.

*3. **Something's Wrong Party.*** Guests at this party must come dressed with a subtle mistake (two different earrings, upside down pin, earrings made out of peas or pearl onions, a paper clip on a tie, unmatched socks, a missing button, half a haircut, slip showing, rip in pants seam, etc.). The house also features mistakes: dead flowers, upside down chair, very dirty window, burned-out light bulbs, crooked pictures, comic books on the coffee table. The food also follows the theme: only spoons to eat with, dessert served first, paper towels as napkins, unmatched glassware and dishes. You may find that many mistakes go unnoticed!

*4. **Flower Power Party.*** One young couple has a springtime potluck dinner when their garden comes into bloom. They purchase inexpensive vases from yard sales and decorate the entire house with bouquets of flowers. At the end of the evening, each guest takes home a vase of flowers.

*5. **The Equestrian Party.*** A family living in the country has an annual summertime horse party. Friends gather at a public stable in the late afternoon for a trail ride to a scenic destination. The horses chosen are docile enough to reassure even the most novice rider. At the stopping place, blankets and picnic cloths are spread and each person is given a red-checked cloth bundle containing a hearty supper of chicken, salad, rolls, beverage, and cake (an extra horse with saddle bags has brought these items). In the twilight, the group sings its way back to the corral.

*6. **Microwave Magic.*** This idea began when microwave ovens were first introduced to the public. The hostess took cooking lessons and also had her teacher come to show off the wonders of these ovens. Even today, a microwave party is a unique way to entertain both men and women. The party is held in the kitchen with stools and chairs for all. Ingredients and instructions for the preplanned menu are ready. Guests are paired off to prepare one course and others watch (and eat) as the appetizer, main dish, vegetable, potatoes, hot beverage, and even the cake proceed into and out of the microwave.

*7. **Mystery Party.*** One of the easiest ways to have a great party is by using one of the mystery party kits available at game stores. These kits provide you with the script, clues, costume ideas, and solution. Each guest has an acting part, but with many guests you can have several people work together as one character. And, you can create an extra role for a reporter who interviews the guests. A group who enjoys dressing up and thinking hard to solve a mystery can really have fun using one of these box games.

*8. **Photographic Progressive Dinner.*** Having to view someone's vacation trip slides can be deadly if you're trapped into seeing hours of pictures in a dark room conducive to sleep. One neighborhood group has the solution: a photographic progressive dinner at the end of summer. Each house serves one course and also shows slides or photos of their recent trip. But, the rule is: no more than twenty slides or ten minutes at a sitting. The party uses five houses (so depending on the size of the families, ten to twenty people attend) and the food assignments are divided into appetizer, soup, salad and rolls, casserole, and dessert.

*9. **Poetry Party.*** When four couples found that literature was something they enjoyed sharing and discovering together, they started a monthly party at one another's homes.

Kids are invited and often join in reading poems they like. As the youngsters have grown, their contributions have changed from Dr. Seuss to Robert Frost. A video in another room provides an alternate activity when the poetry sharing loses its appeal for the younger ones. This party is a way of getting to know people on a different level. Some contributors recite from memory their favorite poems, and all are surprised by the tremendous variety offered.

10. **Puzzle Party.** Everything about this party is puzzling! Start with the written invitations: cut each invitation into about ten pieces and send them off for invitees to receive and assemble.

The guests can be puzzling too. In advance, look up in a name book (available at the library) the meaning of each guest's name. For example, the name *Helen* means "shining light" and the name *Jacob* means "heel grabber." Write all the meanings on a list you'll copy and give to each guest as he arrives, secretly telling each person what his name means. Each person is to identify the others by asking questions such as "Are you like a light bulb?" When the question gets a "yes," the guest writes the name after the meaning.

Next, make the refreshments puzzling. Prepare eight different dips or spreads for crackers and veggies. Place them in different places around the house. Give each guest a paper numbered to eight on which they will try to write the main ingredient of the dip (deviled ham, crab, onion, spinach, peanut butter/jelly, mushroom, green chilis and cheese, olive, shrimp, and peach). Prepare a large punch bowl and make the contents puzzling, too. (A surprising but delicious mixture is apple cider and whipped cream.)

Buy or borrow puzzles of the smaller variety (not those 500-piece monsters!) and place them on separate small tables. Divide the guests into teams of two or three each, and see which group can finish their puzzle first. Of course, their prizes will be puzzles!

PARTY ACTIVITIES

In addition to those activities already explained in the parties described above, the following are more ways to have fun.

Icebreaker. Before the party, write short, outlandish statements on pieces of paper that are given to each guest as they arrive. They are to work the phrase into the predinner conversation—without being caught. Here are some starters: "Can you imagine that this shrimp is fifteen dollars a pound?" "I understand they're having the carpet cleaned after this party." "Have you noticed that she's ignoring him tonight?" At dinner, see who used their phrase and got away unnoticed.

Finding a Partner. Often partners are needed for a game, for dinner, for dancing. Here are three ways of pairing off invitees:
1. Women (or men) leave one shoe in a basket at the door. Men pick a shoe and find the person it belongs to.
2. Men are asked to bring to the party a book or magazine that they enjoy. These are placed on a table, the women select one, and then have to find who it belongs to.
3. Half of the invitees put their middle names on slips of papers in a hat. The other half pull out a name and must find that person by asking a question using their own

middle name: "Hello, I'm George, are you Madeline?" It starts good conversations about names and family backgrounds.

Conversation Starters. For dinner, seat guests at tables of four. Let them choose a topic of community importance to discuss. After dinner, when everyone gathers, one person from each group can share some of their conclusions.

Another way to get people talking during a non-sit-down event is to take guests aside, one at a time, and plant an item on them. Then each invitee is given a slip of paper with the name of an item on it. Attenders thus meet everyone and ask if they have the item. These can be a silver dollar, a broken pencil, a ring, a postage stamp, cologne, a fake fingernail, a toy car, a playing card, and so forth.

Tell the Truth. With a group of twelve or more, each person writes down something that no one else knows about him (excluding spouses). These papers are put in a bowl and then each person selects one. Going around the circle, the person reads the statement and gets one guess as to who has written it. For example, a guest says "Martha, are you the person who dyed her hair red at age fifteen?" (If it's not Martha, you move on to the next person who reads the statement he has and tries to guess who wrote it.) Some interesting truths that have been told include: "I had the male lead in a musical" (it was a woman who attended an all-girls school). "I danced with the grandson of Sitting Bull." "I hate to wear underwear." "I flunked typing twice." "I desperately want another child" (the truth told by a man—and it really surprised his wife!). Sometimes you'll go around the circle several times as guesses are finally correct because the field of possibilities shrinks.

Paper and Pencil Games. Here are four that you can reproduce. Make a copy for each player.

WHIZ QUIZ

Find a pair of rhyming words for each definition.
Examples: Overweight swine=big pig   Mind consuming=brain drain

1. Bug's slacks

2. Unique female horse

3. Recreation area at night

4. Shoe-tying competition

5. Shaky peace agreement

6. Place where clowns train

7. Undetermined disease

8. Watery mirage

9. Psychiatrist's bed for grumps

10. Masculine fowl

11. Wet freeway entry road

12. Penny run over by train

13. Chaise lounge

14. Grin of doe or buck

15. Well-mannered jouster

16. Luggage lost at sea

17. Brother's fat daughter

18. Parisian saucy serving person

19. Kiss just below the chin

20. Independence Day apple pastry

21. Strange facial hair

22. Cost of frozen water

23. Poorly lighted athletic building

24. To borrow homemade liquor

ANSWERS: 1. Ants pants   2. Rare mare   3. Dark park   4. Lace race   5. Loose truce   6. Fool school   7. Vague plague   8. Fake lake   9. Grouch couch   10. Male quail   11. Damp ramp   12. Bent cent   13. French bench   14. Deer leer   15. Polite knight   16. Sunk trunk   17. Obese niece   18. French wench   19. Neck peck   20. July pie   21. Weird beard   22. Ice price   23. Dim gym   24. Mooch hooch

From *The Family Party Book*, copyright © 1996 by Caryl Krueger

A SHELF OF CANS

How many of these "cans" can you name?

1. A can that gives light: _____

2. A can that is sweet: _____

3. A can you can eat: _____

4. A can that's a country: _____

5. A can that lets you delete:_____

6. A can that a horse enjoys:_____

7. A can that's a savage:_____

8. A can that's filled with water: _____

9. A can that is eaten in an Italian restaurant:_____

10. A can used in war: _____

11. A can used in architecture:_____

12. A can that warbles: _____

13. A can that barks: _____

14. A can on the breakfast menu: _____

15. A can played with cards: _____

16. A can that produces packed foods: _____

17. A can to take on a hike:_____

18. A can that is deep and narrow: _____

19. A can at a building entrance: _____

20. A can used by a forthright person: _____

ANSWERS: 1. candle 2. candy 3. canapé 4. Canada 5. cancel 6. canter 7. cannibal 8. canal 9. cannelloni 10. cannon 11. cantilever 12. canary 13. canine 14. cantaloupe 15. canasta 16. cannery 17. canteen 18. canyon 19. canopy 20. candor

THE TASTE TEST

Fill in the blanks with the names of food items.

1. Istanbul is in _____.

2. "Hurry dear, _____ be going."

3. "I'm broke, can you give me a little _____."

4. The _____achian mountains are beautiful this year.

5. The Parthenon is in _____.

6. Some prizefighters get _____ ears.

7. The twentieth letter of the alphabet is _____.

8. Some people don't _____ all about the environment.

9. This food is found in the area of a circle: _____

10. "You are the _____ of the earth."

11. We call two of a kind a _____.

12. She wanted to buy it, _____ husband said "No!"

13. If you step on a tomato, you're apt to _____ it.

14. "I'll _____ you at 6:30 sharp."

15. "She's been down in the dumps so I'll try to _____ up."

16. The angel promised "_____ on earth, goodwill to men."

17. The commercial asked "Where's the _____?"

18. Kids may _____ their noses at food they don't like.

19. In Hawaii, you'll find many people _____ in the sun.

20. Adam and Eve were busy _____ Cain.

ANSWERS: 1. turkey   2. lettuce   3. dough   4. apple   5. grease
6. cauliflower   7. tea   8. carrot   9. pie   10. salt
11. pear   12. butter   13. squash   14. meat   15. pepper
16. peas   17. beef   18. turnip   19. bacon   20. raisin

From *The Family Party Book*, copyright © 1996 by Caryl Krueger

LICENSE PLATES

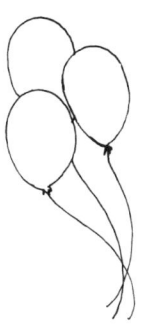

1. EIEIO _____
2. 2DI4 _____
3. 2BRNT2B _____
4. BRBDL _____
5. LADEDA _____
6. YSREBOB _____
7. EZ4ME _____
8. IMWHOIM _____
9. EZ2PLEZ _____
10. EYEMA10 _____
11. HOLIKOW _____
12. OWLBCNU _____
13. EGOPL8 _____
14. ICNTDRV _____
15. GR8D8B8 _____
16. WEBFUT _____
17. AV8OR _____
18. HOLN1 _____
19. 1B1RU12 _____
20. SOSUME _____
21. IXLR8 _____
22. XKWIZIT _____

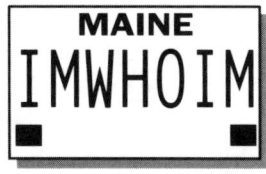

ANSWERS:

1. E-I-E-I-O
2. To die for
3. To be or not to be
4. Barbie doll
5. La de dah
6. Yes siree bob
7. Easy for me
8. I am who I am
9. Easy to please
10. I'm a 10
11. Holy cow
12. I'll be seeing you
13. Ego plate
14. I can't drive
15. Great date bait
16. Web foot
17. Aviator
18. Hole in one
19. I be one. Are you one two?
20. So sue me.
21. I accelerate
22. Exquisite

From *The Family Party Book*, copyright © 1996 by Caryl Krueger

WINNING PARTY RECIPES

Many of my party-giver friends are great cooks, and for your dining pleasure they have shared these easy, make-ahead recipes.

The No-Leftovers Appetizer

This hearty appetizer makes enough for a large party and can be made the day before and heated just before the party begins.

16 ounces imitation crabmeat
3 large (8 oz.) packages cream cheese
1½ cups mayonnaise
1 bunch of green onions, chopped fine
1 teaspoon Worcestershire sauce
1 dash tabasco/hot sauce
1 teaspoon salt
¼ teaspoon pepper

In a large mixing bowl, gently beat the cream cheese, then add all other ingredients except crabmeat. Cream again. Add crabmeat and mix. Pour into two microwavable serving bowls. Heat on high for five minutes (or if using conventional oven, bake for twenty minutes at 350 degrees). Serve with crackers.

Hearty Soup for a Party

Serve in bowls or mugs on a cold night. It's a complete meal in itself when served with salad and garlic bread.

1 pound hamburger (or ground turkey)
1 green pepper
1 onion
2 stalks celery
30 oz. can of tomatoes
30 oz. of water (use can as measure)
1 can kidney beans
1 cup macaroni

Brown hamburger, drain well, and set aside. Sauté green pepper, onion, celery and add to hamburger. In a large pot mix tomatoes and water. Then add hamburger and pepper/onion/celery. Simmer thirty minutes. Add beans and macaroni and cook until macaroni is done, about twenty minutes. Season to taste. Can be made ahead and reheated. Depending on portion size, serves six.

Two-Week Cabbage Salad

Make this at least one day before your party (it keeps up to two weeks in the refrigerator.)

> 1 large head cabbage
> 1 large onion
> 1 large jar pimiento
> 1 green pepper
> ¾ cup vinegar
> 1½ cups sugar
> ¾ cup oil
> 1 teaspoon salt

Grate or chop fine the cabbage, onion, pimiento, and green pepper, and mix together. Bring to a rolling boil the vinegar, sugar, oil, and salt. Pour over the cabbage mixture and cover tightly. Let stand at room temperature for ninety minutes, then mix. Refrigerate for at least twelve hours before serving. Serves six or more.

Chicken Olé

Here's a main dish you make the day before and just heat and serve before your party.

> 8 half chicken breasts, boned and skinned
> 4 tablespoons butter (divided)
> ½ cup water
> 1 cube chicken bouillon dissolved in one cup hot water
> 12 corn tortillas, sliced into one-inch strips
> 1 can cream of mushroom soup
> 2 cans cream of chicken soup
> 1 six-ounce can of green chili salsa
> 1 onion, grated
> ¾ cup milk
> ½ pound Monterey Jack cheese, grated
> Salt and pepper to taste
> 1 cube chicken bouillon dissolved in one cup hot water

Melt three tablespoons butter in large pan suitable for oven cooking. Salt and pepper chicken. As butter begins to brown, add half cup of water and the chicken. Bake uncovered at 350 degrees for thirty minutes or until cooked, depending on thickness. (You can also bake chicken in the microwave or by your own method.)

While chicken is baking, butter a large casserole using the fourth tablespoon of butter. Next, put one quarter cup of the bouillon/water mixture in the bottom of the casserole. (You will use the remainder if the sauce mixture seems too thick.) In a bowl, mix soups, milk, salsa, and grated onion. When chicken is done, break it into bite-size pieces. Alternate layers of tortillas, chicken, and sauce, making three layers of each. Top with grated cheese and refrigerate for twenty-four hours. Bake at 300 degrees for sixty to ninety minutes until bubbly and heated through. Serves ten to twelve.

The Volcano Cake

Here's an exciting cake for your South Seas Island party (or any other party). And, it's easy to make.

> 6 cake rounds (3 cake mixes or 3 cookbook recipes)
> Double recipe of chocolate frosting
> Double recipe of white frosting
> Green food coloring
> Small juice glass
> Aluminum foil
> White of one egg
> 2 teaspoons sugar
> Red food coloring
> Small quantity of dry ice chunks (handle with gloves,
>   buy the day of the party at an ice-cream store and
>   keep well-wrapped in your freezer)
> Hot water

Bake a triple recipe of your favorite cake. Using about half of the white frosting between the layers, assemble (on a large platter) four of the layers to form a mountain. You do this by trimming each layer a little smaller than the preceding one (save the scraps for snacking). Before assembling the top two layers which you also trim, use the juice glass to cut a hole in the center of each layer. Then place these two layers on top of the other layers with frosting between them. Line the hole with a double layer of foil, making a well, using the glass as a mold. Frost the cake with lots of the chocolate frosting. Next, mix the green food coloring with the remaining white frosting and use it to highlight the chocolate frosting as if it were running down the mountainsides. Don't be stingy with the frosting on your mountain.

Just before serving, make the lava by beating the egg white with the sugar and a few drops of red food coloring, only until it is foamy, not stiff. Now, put small chunks of the dry ice into the foil-lined well of the cake. Pour in the egg mixture and carry the cake to the table. Using very hot water, add about two ounces of water to the well.

Watch the lava and smoke appear as your volcano erupts! This cake will serve twenty-four to thirty.

* * * *

The following chapters describe parties for children of all ages and you'll find that some of the games for older kids are quite adaptable to adult parties. Also read chapters 7 and 8, which have ideas for special occasion entertaining and for no occasion at all—just when you want to party. So start your plans this week!

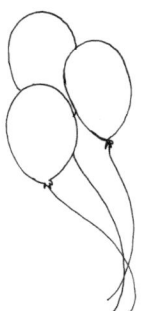

4
Perfect Parties for Preschoolers

Until a toddler's third birthday, children's parties are mainly occasions for parents to show off the little darling to family and friends. It's usually an affair with cake, ice cream, and a few presents, but not a real child-oriented party. In fact, babies have little idea of what's going on and may fuss through the entire event. So, you might as well admit that these parties are for you, the parent.

However, when a child is to be three, a simple party can be lots of fun. The parties described in this chapter are for children three to six years of age.

TIPS TO MAKE THE PARTY RUN SMOOTHLY

* Let the child invite as many friends as her age (a three-year-old invites three others, a six-year-old invites six others). This is a manageable-size party and the most fun. Including extra adults, you could have as many as ten or twelve in attendance, but for these early ages, smaller is usually better.

* For three-year-olds, invite the moms and/or dads to come, too. At this age the child is sometimes shy and feels more comfortable with a parent nearby.

* Consider putting on the invitation "Please, no gifts." In this materialistic society, it is refreshing for your guests to know that the party will be an opportunity to celebrate fun and friendship. For one-, two-, and three-year-olds, gifts don't have much importance. Moms who have tried this report that no one missed the gift opening.

* Two hours in length is ideal. Put the time on the invitation: "From 3:00 to 5:00 in the afternoon." And for happy and rested guests, remember to avoid naptimes.

* Specify on the invitation the kind of apparel that will be appropriate: party clothes, play clothes, swimsuits and robes.

* Mail invitations, rather than having a child, parent, or teacher hand them out at day care or play school where those not invited will have hurt feelings. A mailed invitation gets the attention of the parent.

* Put RSVP in big letters so you'll know how many youngsters (and adults) will be coming.

* A well-planned home party can be just as much fun as a more expensive party at a special restaurant or entertainment facility. Remember, you'll be giving many parties for this child and there will be opportunities for more elaborate events in subsequent years. We know a toddler who was brought to his party in the park via limousine! Save that for later—or better yet, never.

* Involve the birthday child in the planning. You may want to test some of the activities on her in advance to be sure they are age-suitable.

* Prepare your child in advance concerning good manners: greeting guests, sharing toys, being a good sport, opening packages and thanking for them, and saying good-bye to friends.

* Plan a first event, an icebreaker, that can be started as the guests arrive. Often a toy, such as a train set or playhouse, is sufficient.

* Choose activities where every youngster will feel successful. Children this age are not adept at competing for prizes. Applause, claps, or shouts of "hooray!" are sufficient awards. But if you have prizes, be sure that each child gets one.

* Serve food where spills don't matter. In good weather, an outdoor deck or patio that can be hosed off afterward is ideal. For indoors, set the kids' table in an entry hall with a tile floor, in the playroom, or on top of a big colorful sheet or tarpaulin.

* Plan the party with a time schedule, estimating the length of time for each activity. (To give you an example, I've included such a schedule in one of the parties in this chapter.) By doing this there will be no "What do we do now?" surprises. Have an extra activity in mind should the party go faster than you'd planned. Playing tag in the yard, dancing to music, watching a kid video, doing somersaults, or playing hide-and-go-seek can fill up that extra time.

* Plan a take-home item so that each child goes home with something in hand.

* If your child is a guest at a party, be sure to pick him up promptly at the ending time. The host family will appreciate your consideration.

THE TOP FIVE KID-TESTED PARTIES

1. The Pirate Party

Cartoons and books have made most young children quite aware of pirates. One party-giver shared the video of *Peter Pan* in advance of the party, sending it around to each home.

GUESTS: This party works well for a mixture of boys and girls between four and six years of age. It accommodates more youngsters (ten were invited) than a typical party, but remember my suggestion for one guest for each year of the child's age. You will need five adults to help.

THEME: The house becomes a pirate ship. "Pirate coves" are created for activities that are staffed by the adults.

LENGTH OF PARTY: All the activities fit into two hours.

INVITATION: Using brown paper grocery bags, tear out large pieces, write party details, then crumple them into treasure maps with an X marking the spot—the address for the party.

DECOR: A homemade pirate flag in front of the house is all that's needed. (Children this age are too short to notice most high-up decorations such as streamers.)

ACTIVITIES/GAMES: This party, which started at 10:30 A.M. is carefully charted as follows:

10:30—Arrivals. Guests gather in living room to decorate premade newspaper pirate hats with pirate stickers. Each child is also given a bag with her name on it for the little items she will collect. When all have arrived, the pirate story is told, a story that describes all the events in the pirate coves. Each youngster is given an eye patch and made an official pirate.

10:50—Pirate cove activities begin. The children are paired off and then each pair has an adult to take them to one specific pirate cove in the house. Every five minutes, a "ship's bell" is rung, indicating that they go to the next cove. (Put a numbered pirate flag at each of the five coves and start each pair at a different number, telling the adult guide to rotate the youngsters to the next higher number, except for those at cove five, who rotate to cove one.) The coves are as follows:

1. **Buried Treasure.** In the playroom is a tent filled with pillows and stuffed animals. Leading to the tent is a tunnel (made from card tables covered with sheets). Each pair of youngsters goes through the tunnel to the tent, looking for buried treasure (hidden wrapped candy gold coins if possible). After each pair exits, the supply of candy in the tent is replenished by the adult. (Figure about five candies per child.)

2. **Pirate Bottle Knockers.** In another room, there is a black-draped ironing board with cans on it. The two children take turns throwing beanbags at the cans to knock them over. The accompanying adult keeps setting up the cans and handing back the beanbags until the bell rings. Then, each child receives stickers as a prize.

3. **Pirate Fishing.** In the doorway to another room, a sheet is fastened securely across the door opening at about a five-foot height. With homemade fishing poles with string attached, show youngsters how to cast their string over the sheet. An adult on the other side sometimes clips a paper fish onto the line, but at least once he clips a small bag of goldfish crackers onto the fishing line. Kids continue to fish until the bell rings.

45

4. **Walk the Plank.** In the living room (or out on the lawn), place a long plank at least five feet long. (A two-by-four works well.) The youngsters take turns walking the length of the board. Next, each tries to walk the plank while balancing a book on her head, then while holding a partner's hand, and finally walking it blindfolded. When the bell rings, plank walkers receive pirate pencils (pencils with pirate stickers on them).

5. **String 'Em Up.** In another room, have tables with marking pens, stickers, string, and cardboard precut in the shape of large medals. Each child makes a pirate medallion and hangs it around his neck. (You might make one ahead as an example.)

11:15—Sink or swim. This is played by all children together in a large room. Play up-beat music so that the pirates can dance as if they are swimming, moving their arms vigorously. When the music is suddenly stopped, they must sink to the floor. While you can play that the last one to fall to the floor is out, most youngsters like to just keep playing.

11:25—Meanwhile, an adult has hidden ten treasure packages labeled with each guest's name around the house. Children join with a partner and an adult guide. Each pair is given a simple map of the house with an X on it, showing where their treasures are hidden. When they have found their treasures, they return to the party room to open their treasure adventure kits to find items such as a compass, canteen, flashlight, child binoculars, and so forth. (Be sure to put batteries in items requiring them.)

11:40—Pirate's lunch: Hot dogs (called pirate dogs), deep-fried mozzarella (called gooey fish bait—a wonderful food that one adult can prepare during the party for you), and grapes in whipped cream (called eyeballs in sauce).

11:55—Cake time. Make a sheet cake and decorate it with a pirate ship. Serve with ice cream.

12:10—Gift opening

12:25—Pirate's farewell. Using the sofa as a pirate ship, let all youngsters climb on board. Place the plank, used earlier, as a ramp from the sofa to the floor. As a parent arrives, his child walks down the plank to leave.

PLANNING AHEAD: Other than the simple food, you'll need to make the invitations, pirate flags, pirate hats, fishing poles, and treasure maps, set up the five pirate coves, obtain a bell, the eye patches, and items for the adventure kits, plus the little rewards given at the five coves.

2. *The Dress-up Party*

Little girls love to dress up in grown-up clothes and high heels, so this party is a real winner.

GUESTS: This works best with three to six little girls. One mom tried it with two boys as part of the group and she said they enjoyed dressing up in male adult clothes. However, an all-girls party is recommended.

THEME: Dressing up and having a tea party. You will want to look in your own closet, visit a thrift shop, or borrow from friends in order to gather dress-up clothing. You'll need a dress for each child (these should be about three sizes too big), high heels, hats and trimmings, and handbags.

LENGTH OF PARTY: Two hours.

INVITATION: Even though most of the guests don't read yet, send an elegant written invitation. With kid help, make these by decorating the paper with catalog pictures of fancily dressed women.

DECOR: The low tea table with linens, dishes, and flower centerpiece can be placed where it will be seen and admired.

ACTIVITIES/GAMES (and approximate time needed)

1. **Icebreaker** (ten minutes). As guests arrive, invite them to sit on the floor in a circle and make pasta necklaces. Have a bowl of uncooked thick, colored noodles and yarn for stringing. (If you don't know how to color noodles, see #94 in chapter 10.) The noodles thread easily if the end of the yarn is wrapped in tape. Allow time for each child to make at least one necklace.

2. **Dress-up Time** (fifteen minutes). In a large box, have the dresses and shoes, plus other items such as scarves, ties, and lengths of material (which are a favorite for wrapping around head and body). Encourage the youngsters to try on several different dresses and combinations before settling on one.

3. **The Hat Hunt** (ten minutes). Before the party, hide hats for each child in different rooms of the house. The hats can be partly hidden or placed on large stuffed animals and dolls. If you can't find inexpensive used hats, purchase plain straw hats that you can trim or let the girls decorate.

4. **Photo Time** (five minutes). With gowns, necklaces, heels, and hats, let each youngster be a model. Have a little bench for the child to stand on and pose in front of a mirror. Take an instant photo of each dressed-up girl to take home.

5. **Dress-up Tea Party** (twenty minutes). Let the dressed-up girls sit at their own special table. Serve miniature foods: fruits on short skewers, tiny sandwiches or mini-quiche (which can be bought frozen and ready to heat), and miniature cupcakes with a candle on each. If possible, have a tea set or use demitasse cups for fruit juice "tea." Using a cream pitcher, provide additional "tea" that they can pour themselves. (Pouring is a very popular activity!)

6. **Cake Time** (ten minutes). While the miniature cupcakes may be sufficient, for a birthday party have a larger cake with candles so everyone can sing "Happy Birthday."

7. **Gift Time** (ten minutes). Some help may be needed for younger children to open packages. A helping parent can read the card to identify the giver, and keep a list of the gifts.

8. **Dress-up the Doll** (ten minutes). In advance, using shelf paper or other large paper, draw a doll about the same size as the guest of honor. Draw on simple shorts and shirt, but no other clothing. Tape it to a door or wall. Out of colored paper, cut clothes (about ten pieces): blouse, skirt, hat, purse, two mittens, two socks, two boots. Let youngsters choose the piece they want to put on the paper doll. If parents are present, let them also choose clothing to put on the doll. Use a scarf to blindfold the participants (parents first and then the youngsters) as they attempt to get the clothing pieces in the right places. Have a regular scarf for adults, and a sheer scarf for the youngsters. This will permit the children to see a little and get the items in the correct places. As they place the clothing on the doll, tape it in place. You'll come up with some unique locations (like a mitten on the head) and the girls will also laugh at their parent's inability to get the clothing where it belongs.

9. **Hide-and-Seek** (fifteen minutes). Using the entire house (unless a room door is closed), let the mothers hide. After two minutes, let the girls go and find their mothers. At one party where grandmothers were also invited, the grandmas hid first, then the moms looked for them and hid with them, and finally the girls went in search of both mom and grandma.

10. **The "Take Home"** (ten minutes). Before the party, pack secondhand purses with goodies. Contents can include: tablet, pen, ring, fan, rubber stamp, bracelet, comb, lip gloss, small book, puzzle, fake money. You can find these inexpensive items at bargain stores. The purses can be hidden in one room and the guests get to take home the one they find first. Allow time for letting the guests look through the purse contents.

FOOD: The cupcakes and cake can be made and frosted the day before. The quiches or sandwiches and fruit skewers can be made the day of the party. Have orangeade or apple juice as the fake tea.

PRIZES: The purses and their contents.

ADVANCE PREPARATION: Other than preparing the tea table and the food, you'll need to locate the clothing, accessories, hats, and purses. Prepare the dress-up doll and the materials for necklace making. Collect all the items for the purses. Don't forget the instant camera and film.

3. The Snowball Party

When you must have a party during snow season, here's one that little folks will enjoy. However, one family living in a warm climate had a hit party because they had a load of artificial snow dumped in their yard.

GUESTS: Four to eight boys and girls five to six years old is ideal, but it can also work for younger kids.

THEME: Everything to do with snow: sleds, Eskimos, snowballs, snow angels, and warm clothes. It can be held in a house with yard or adapted to a park with a warming house or heated pavilion.

LENGTH OF PARTY: Two hours for three- and four-year-olds, or up to three hours for five- and six-year-olds.

INVITATION: Snowflake invitations can be made by folding white paper and then cutting it, being careful to leave the center intact where the party information can be lettered.

DECOR: Make an indoors snowman. Cut an old white sheet into three squares: large, medium, and small. Put rumpled newspapers into the center of each square, then draw the corners together and tie with string, making three balls. Stack them up like a snowman. With an old hat and marking pens, decorate him.

For a wonderful table centerpiece, make an igloo out of rectangular sugar cubes. Cover the centerpiece area with cotton except for an eight-inch circle where the igloo will be. Prepare two egg whites beaten with three cups of powdered sugar to use as mortar. Make the first circle of cubes, leaving a space for the entrance. Make each succeeding circle a little smaller, staggering the cubes, and working from the entrance toward the back. You'll want to make your igloo about ten rows high. Then make a curved entrance tunnel and mortar it in place. Make a cardboard roof and cover it with cubes. If it's an evening party, a very small flashlight placed inside your igloo makes it glow.

ACTIVITIES/GAMES:

1. **Icebreaker.** In advance, make an igloo by covering a round card table with a white sheet. Extend the sheet outward on one side to make the igloo entrance. Let guests pretend to be Eskimos and crawl in and out of the igloo until everyone has arrived. See how many Eskimos can fit inside the igloo.

2. **Hot, Warm, Cold.** Prepare in advance, one for each child, a sealed plastic bag with an ice cube inside. Put these in an ice bucket at the start of the game. The group sits in a circle with one adult who has a stopwatch. One child is told to go into another room while a bagged ice cube is hidden. She is then called back into the room and must search for it. When found, the number of minutes it took is noted, and she is the one to hide the next ice cube. The shortest time wins. Kids can be encouraging by calling out "hot," "warm," or "cold."

3. **Find the North Pole.** Establish a starting line and let the kids sit behind it. Put your North Pole (a yardstick in a pail) about ten feet from the line. Have each child's name on a sticker. Blindfold the first child, turn him around several times and then tell him to walk to the spot where he thinks the North Pole is (with a time limit of ten seconds). When he reaches the spot, he is to put his head down on the floor and the adult puts his name sticker at that point. The child who comes the closest to the North Pole wins.

4. **Outside Action.** Now it's time for snow clothes and out into the yard. If the snow is fresh, let kids make snow angels. Play games such as rolling a small snowball toward a marker. In advance of the party, pile snow into a little slope for sliding down. If there's enough snow, you can also make a snowman. With a sled and ropes, play "Rudolph and Santa": children take turns being reindeer and pulling the sled, or sitting behind and being pulled around the yard.

5. **Picture Lotto** (the last game). After inside lunch (and gift opening if it's a birthday party), it's nice to have a game to play as parents arrive. In advance, cut out of magazines a total of twelve small pictures of cold weather scenes, animals like reindeer, and equipment like sleds or skates. Using rubber cement, lightly stick six pictures on one piece of letter-size paper and photocopy it. Then, change the pictures around, removing some and adding different ones, and copy it again. Make a different page for each invitee. Put the twelve original pictures in a bag. Out of construction paper, cut squares (six times the number of guests) that will be used to cover the picture squares. Put these within easy reach of the players. Explain to the children that you will take a picture out of the bag and show it. If the child has that picture, he will cover it with a colored square. Although lotto games have as winner the first one who covers all the squares, most children will want to continue playing until everyone has "won." (And then they may want to play again.)

FOOD: When youngsters come in from the cold, have warm foods ready. Consider pizza, hot dogs, grilled cheese sandwiches, corn on the cob (available frozen), hot apple juice or chocolate, and marshmallows for roasting in the fireplace. Dessert can be cupcakes shaped like snowballs and frosted with coconut.

PRIZES: Since kids often lose mittens, find inexpensive knit mittens to give as the take-home gift. Popsicle molds can be given as prizes for the games.

PLANNING AHEAD: This party requires some advance work, but much can be done well ahead of party day with your youngster's help. Make invitations, snowman, and sugar-cube centerpiece. Then gather outside play equipment, materials for the inside igloo, and the essentials for the ice cube, North Pole, and lotto games. Buy prizes. Food can be made on party day.

4. The Artist Party

Little children love to draw—with crayons, pens, and paints. This party lets them do it all! Read on to see how to manage young artists.

GUESTS: Four to ten five- and six-year-olds is ideal, but you can adapt it for younger kids.

THEME: Art to make, art games, artistic food, art prizes.

LENGTH OF PARTY: Two to three hours.

INVITATION: Make these in the shape of an artist's palette. Tell guests to wear play clothes and a beret style hat.

DECOR: For the front door area or entry hall, make a giant paintbrush angled into a paint can. The brush is made from an old broom by trimming the brush end to a point. Make a large plastic container into a paint pot. Paint the inside of the container and make "drips" down the outside. Paint the broom bristles half way up. Angle the giant brush into the pot.

ACTIVITIES/GAMES:

1. **Icebreaker:** As guests arrive, have a table where you have placed a white T-shirt to be given to the guest of honor. With permanent marking pens, let each child outline his hand on the front or back sides of the shirt that is already labeled: "Happy Birthday from a Handful of Friends."

2. **Blindfold Portraits:** Cover a pair of doors or a wall with paper suitable for drawing, making it long rather than high. Have wide marking pens in various colors. Tell youngsters they are going to make a picture of how they look at the party. For example, ask Katie how she will draw herself. She may say "with black hair and a red shirt and shorts." Next blindfold her, give her the correct color marking pens and let her draw herself. Continue with each child (or two at a time) until you have a complete mural of everyone at the party.

3. **The Artists' Fence.** In advance of the party, buy used plain white T-shirts in a sufficiently large size that they will cover the guests from neck to knees (like an artist's smock). Have ribbons or belts available to tie them on. On a fence outside, affix large pieces of drawing paper, one for each child. Staple small paper cups of various poster paints and water at each location. Let artists go to work drawing anything they choose. You may not need them, but have a few simple suggestions handy ("Draw yourself at the zoo," "Paint your family in a car") for those needing ideas. When the artists are finished, use handwipes for painty fingers and then just fold the T-shirts up on themselves and over the head, leaving clothing clean. (Painting outside is best since paint spills don't matter, but if the weather doesn't permit, set up your painting area on a patio, in the basement, or in the family room with a large dropcloth on the floor.)

4. **Art Hunt.** While the youngsters are painting outside, hide many small art supplies around the house: chalk, paints, brushes, rolls of paper, stickers, individual big crayons, coloring books, pens, and so forth. Have duplicates of popular items. Divide the group into teams of two. Give each pair a bag for what they find and at the word "Go!" let them all start hunting. However, each team must hold hands. When you think everything has been found, call them back into a circle and let them show what they have found. Put all the items in the middle of the circle. Provide a labeled bag for each child. Then, go around the circle, each child choosing one item to take home. Have enough small items that you can go around the circle several times.

5. **Window Painting.** This can be the last event before going home. A sliding glass door is ideal for window painting from the outside. If the weather isn't good, paint it from the inside, but put plenty of paper on the floor. Wearing the T-shirt smocks again, let them paint with fingers, each choosing one color of fairly thick poster paint. Have a big bowl of sudsy water and towels handy. Let them all work together, stopping only as parents come to pick them up. You'll be amazed how nice the glass looks with all the colors on it. (When you're tired of it, it's even fun for your child to wash it off with soapy water.)

FOOD: The food should be in bright poster colors: red, blue, green, yellow. Ask a bakery to make a loaf of bright green bread (or make it at home by adding a little food coloring to the dough). Use red jam for the sandwiches. Have blue Jello. Make cupcakes that are yellow with green frosting. Serve red juice. Instead of a table cloth, cover the table with poster paper that has been finger-painted by your child in advance.

PRIZES/FAVORS: Each guest will take home his bag of art supplies. Guests can also take home their painting T-shirt and the picture they made on the fence.

PLANNING AHEAD: This party doesn't require much advance work: making the entry decoration, buying at a crafts store all the art supplies, getting the birthday T-shirt and the used T-shirts, and preparing the food (which can all be made the day before).

5. *The Animal Party*

Kids love animals and this party will satisfy their desire to hold and pet them. This is not a party at a zoo, but rather a party at a small facility such as a family farm, dairy farm, bird farm, or animal reserve. Call in advance to find a facility that permits hands-on with some animals. Many of these are free. Also inquire if there is a place to picnic nearby, and what animals, such as ducks, can be fed by the youngsters.

GUESTS: With other parents helping, this can be a large party. It is also a party where older or younger siblings fit in nicely.

THEME: Getting to know the animal world.

LENGTH OF PARTY: Two or three hours.

INVITATIONS: From magazines, cut pictures of animals and paste these on pieces of cardboard. Punch each with a hole through which you thread a twenty-four inch length of yarn. Choose animals that make distinctive sounds (dogs, cats, mice, lions, elephants, birds). Put specific details of the party on the back of the cardboard. Remind each invitee to wear her animal card around her neck when she comes to the party.

DECOR: Balloons to indicate your gathering location at the park or farm.

Please note: Balloons can be a hazard for children. Balloons should not be put in the mouth, or given to children under the age of three.

ACTIVITIES/GAMES:

1. **Icebreaker.** As guests arrive wearing their animal cards, they join a circle of children and one parent. The parent tells the group that they are to only speak in animal talk, and lets them practice what their animal says. Then the parent asks questions like: "Is the bear here?" (If he is, he growls.) "Is the bird sitting in the circle?" "Are the mouse and the cat here?" When all the guests are present, it's time for the real animals.

2. **Animal Visits.** Depending on the place, your group will either go to the individual stalls or the animals will be brought out to a viewing area. For example, a handler will usually hold a rabbit or calf so it can be petted. Some goats are also tame enough to be petted. Move slowly enough so that each youngster has the opportunity to see and to touch.

3. **Front and Back.** In advance, cut pictures of animals in half. While lunch is being prepared, put the rear half-picture of each animal on the grass, and give each child a front half. Let them find the match for their half-picture.

4. **Lunchtime for Ducks.** One animal party was held at a farm that had a pond with lots of ducks. After lunch, each youngster was given a bag of stale bread pieces. An adult supervised the feeding since some ducks can be a bit aggressive. Every youngster got to feed ducks (however one youngster was seen eating the bread himself!).

5. **Follow the Animal** (the going home event). Kids line up with an adult in the lead (to set the example). The leader will pretend to be an animal (a hopping

kangaroo, a galloping horse, a monkey with swinging arms, a creeping cat, a dancing dog). Each child chooses an animal he wants to be and practices what he'll do when leader. Then the leader starts to move around in a large circle, or in and out among the trees, with all children following his example. When a whistle is blown, the leader goes to the end of the line and the new child leader starts to act out his animal as he goes around in the circle. This continues until all youngsters have been leader.

FOOD: Pack picnic lunches in bags tied inside large red-checked napkins. Using large cookie cutters, make sandwiches in animal shapes. Include in each bag some fish-shaped crackers, the monkey's banana, and a boxed fruit drink. Make a bunny cake for dessert. (This is easily made with two round layers. One is the bunny head, the other layer is cut into two curved ears and a bow tie. Frost the cake as a brown or white bunny with frosting features and licorice whiskers. The cake transports nicely on a foil-covered tray.)

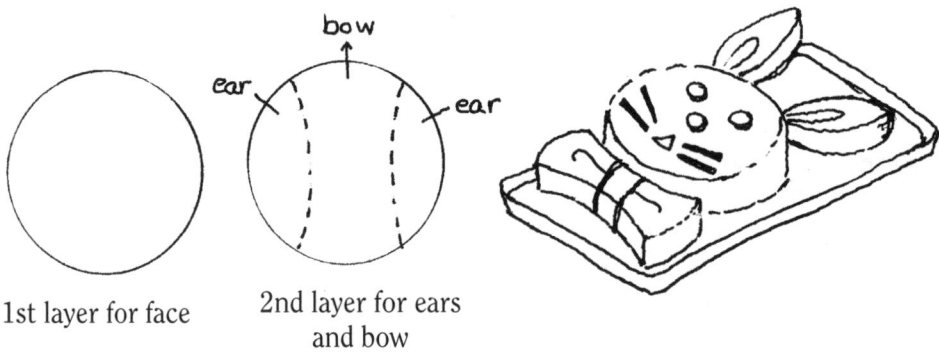

1st layer for face 2nd layer for ears and bow

PRIZES/FAVORS: At going home time, have little bags of favors ready. Items should tie-in with the animal theme: stickers, books, animal cookies, self-inking animal stamps, animal masks.

PLANNING AHEAD: Once you've located the right place, this party isn't a lot of work. The invitations, balloons, half-animal pictures, take-home bags, the bread bags for feeding ducks, the lunches, and cake are not last-minute items and all transport well. Remember to take along handwipes and several large garbage bags for easy clean up.

FIVE MORE FUN THEMES

Let these additional ideas spark your own creative plans.

1. **The Circus Party.** If you don't want to hire a clown, be one! Kids love clown antics and tricks. Decorate with balloons. Borrow or make clown, animal, and trainer costumes. Do somersaults and handstands. Walk a rope on the floor. Let children pretend to be lions and the trainer.

2. **The Fairy Tale Party.** Choose a fairy tale for each of the guests. Read the story, using her name as one of the characters. Have some simple costumes to go with the stories. Since this involves sitting, let the games be active relay races.

3. **The Train Party.** From friends and neighbors, collect several easy-to-run wooden train sets (like Brio) suitable for young children. Have train hats and whistles as kids make new layouts. Set up chairs on either side of a long hallway and pretend it is a train complete with tickets and stops, plus kids as engineer and conductor. Cut a sheet cake into rectangular pieces and decorate these like train cars.

4. **Sports Party.** For a summer party, celebrate child athletics. Make an obstacle course. Have a beam to jump over or climb under. Ride bikes on the patio. Use all the backyard equipment. Play kickball or backyard soccer. Play badminton with a net, rackets, and Nerf balls. Play many relay races. Cook lunch outside on the barbecue: hot dogs, sweet corn, and serve juice drinks.

5. **The Wizard of Oz Party.** Five- and six-year-olds usually know this story, but don't hesitate to retell it or show part of the video to start the party. You'll need a basement or garage for the event. Using yellow chalk, make a circuitous yellow brick road leading to Oz. On the way, stop at Munchkin Land (where kids pick lollipops off a fake tree), the Emerald City (where they have their picture taken in a green light), and play games with the Scarecrow (throwing beanbags at his hat), the Tin Man (where they're blindfolded and try to pin a heart on his cutout), and the Lion (where they have a "Who can roar the loudest" contest). Play hopscotch on the yellow brick road after a lunch of Munchkin food (little sandwiches, little fruit such as grapes, little chips, little carrot strips, little cookies, little glasses of milk).

SIX GOOD GAMES AND ACTIVITIES

1. **The Penny Hunt.** In the yard, scatter one hundred pennies. Give a bag to each youngster and see who can find the most in five minutes. Count up the pennies and if it doesn't total one hundred, send the hunters out once more.

2. **The Tunnel.** At a fabric shop buy a twelve-foot length of stretchy black tube material. (This is usually a seamless jersey fabric.) The investment will last you for years and can be an integral part of games for youngsters as well as adults. Little kids will use it as a tunnel, teens will play relay races through it, family parties can team up a parent and child going opposite directions and having to pass each other inside the tunnel. It helps if an adult holds each end.

3. **Cookie Decorating.** At holiday times, let kids put the finishing touches on pre-made plain sugar cookies: hearts, pumpkins, Christmas trees, and so forth. Families can also decorate cookies for a contest for the best decorated—and then eat them. For variety, you can give the kids some unbaked cookie dough to form into people and animals—then bake these on a cookie sheet.

4. **Musical Balloons.** Rather than musical chairs, play the same game with balloons—buy the sturdier kind that won't break easily. Place one fewer balloon than players in the middle of the room. Players circle the balloons and when the music stops they must sit on one. Young children are usually not heavy enough to break the balloons, but do have extras in case some get broken along the way.

5. **Pin the . . .** You can create wonderful variations on the old "Pin the Tail on the Donkey" game. All you need is paper, markers, a blindfold, and pins. Try "Pin the Scales on the Stegosaurus" and "Pin the Spots on the Dalmatian" (both great for the smallest kids since scales and spots can go anywhere) or "Pin the Beak on the Parrot," or "Pin the Bucket on the Skiploader" (a favorite of little boys).

6. **Beanbags.** Make simple bags out of remnants and fill with navy beans for use in a variety of ways. You'll use these for many parties over many years. They can be the anchor for a cluster of helium balloons at the center of the table. Use them as take-home party favors. Make a beanbag toss game by drawing a teddy bear with a big cut-out mouth on posterboard and then letting kids take turns tossing beanbags through the hole. Or have races letting kids crawl with a beanbag balanced on their backs.

FIVE TASTY AND EASY-TO-MAKE PARTY FOODS

1. **Waffles and pancakes.** Rather than serving sandwiches, make these in advance, then warm them and serve with toppings such as strawberries, bananas in whipped cream, or chocolate sauce.

2. **Sprinkles.** While not technically a food, they give many foods a festive look. You can save money by purchasing a large container of them at a food discount store. Use them with dishes of yogurt or cereal, on cupcakes or ice cream. One party-giver reports that her son introduced his friends to cooked hot dogs with sprinkles!

3. **Basket of food.** Forget plates. Fill individual baskets with foil-wrapped finger foods: chicken pieces, pineapple chunks, carrot sticks, buttered roll, cookies. Baskets transport easily and also make nice take-home gifts.

4. **Pig in a blanket.** These are much easier to eat than hot dogs in buns. Just wind refrigerated crescent biscuit dough around the hot dogs and bake. You can even put a little cheese and catsup inside. No leftover ends of buns!

5. **Sundaes.** Let kids create their own sundaes with assorted ice creams, syrups, toppings, and whipped cream. Give each youngster a large dinner plate for assembling his creation in the shape of a face or animal.

* * *

You may wish to look in chapter 5, parties for grade-schoolers, to find ideas you can adapt to preschool children.

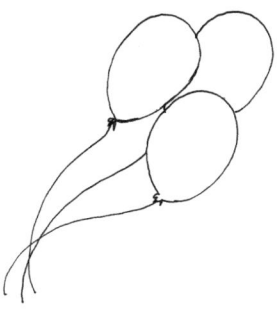

5
Grade School Get-Togethers

Parties for grade-schoolers are usually as enjoyable for the adult hosts as for the youngsters because these kids are old enough to appreciate a party theme and to follow more elaborate game instructions. Yet they aren't so sophisticated that they won't partake in silly fun. For youngsters seven through twelve, going to a party is still a big deal!

TIPS TO MAKE THE PARTY RUN SMOOTHLY

* Plan an icebreaker game for the first event. This should be an activity that includes guests as they arrive, and lasts until everyone is present.
* Mix girls and boys at a party if the theme permits (slumber parties are exceptions!). Usually the two sexes are together in most school classes and are not self-conscious about being together at a social event.
* Don't let the party activities lag so that guests splinter into cliques; keep the events moving right along. This age prefers action to socializing.
* If possible, have only one other adult help you run the party. Grade-schoolers are often good party assistants and the guest of honor can be primed to manage certain events.
* Prizes are very important for this age group. Have lots of them and be sure everyone carries something home.
* In competitions, rarely let it be the girls versus the boys. And since these youngsters are far more competitive than preschoolers, be alert to unfair tactics being used to win.

* Plan plenty of hearty snacks and food. You can always feed leftovers to the family or freeze them for later.
* Make the invitation very clear, especially if a costume is involved. Underline the RSVP line and explain in writing what it means so youngsters can add this skill to their good manners.

THE FIVE TOP KID-TESTED PARTIES

1. The Safari Party

GUESTS: Anywhere from seven to fifteen youngsters are manageable for this party, ideal for youngsters ages seven through ten. Safari clothes should be worn (khakis, jeans, colorful shirts, pith helmets, dark glasses, boots, backpacks, binoculars).

THEME: The magic and mystery of the jungle safari comes alive in your family room, backyard, or nearby park. You can get many of the supplies and prizes for this party at any army surplus store.

LENGTH OF PARTY: About three hours.

INVITATION: Use pictures of off-road vehicles easily found in newspaper ads. Paste them on colorful paper and add the details, including what to wear. One party-giver found a Jeep dealership happy to give her brochures that had great pictures she could use.

DECOR: Give the entrance (door or gate) a jungle look with green crepe paper twisted into vines and hung straight down from the top of the door frame or tree so that guests must enter through the vines. In the party room or out in the yard, place stuffed "jungle" animals looking down at the party from shelves or tree branches. Hang climbing ropes from trees—a fun activity for anytime during the party.

ACTIVITIES/GAMES:

1. **Icebreaker: Feed the Elephant** (twenty minutes). Using the cardboard center from a roll of paper towels, cover most of it with gray paper, but cover about two inches at one end with pink paper. As guests arrive, they receive three unshelled peanuts and join in the game. First ask if anyone knows what the paper roll is. If they're stumped, tell them that you couldn't fit an entire elephant through the door so you just brought his trunk.

Make a string circle only six feet in diameter. Youngsters sit behind the string with one child seated in the center, holding the trunk on his forehead (not over his mouth or nose) pointed at the ceiling. When you shout "There's an elephant, give him a peanut!" each youngster tosses a peanut toward the trunk. The elephant can not move his head and trunk or move from his seated position. The first youngster to get a peanut down the trunk becomes the next elephant and the game starts over.

2. **The Lion's Tail** (fifteen minutes). In advance, make a simple tail from yellow cloth with a knot at the end. Seat the participants in a circle. The guest of honor tucks the tail into the back of her waistband and circles the outside of the seated group, tapping each child on the shoulder and saying "Lion." Then, she touches one player and says "Hyena!" This child jumps up and chases the lion, who must dash around the circle and sit in the hyena's place before the hyena can grab her tail. If the hyena snatches the lion's tail, the lion remains the lion. However if the hyena cannot snatch it, the hyena becomes the new "king of the jungle."

3. **Jungle Treasure Hunt** (thirty minutes). Prepare written clues for a treasure hunt (indoors, outside, or both). Examples: Find a watering hole in the jungle (the bathtub or birdbath). Go where the jungle natives dry their animal hides (the oven). Search for the place a not-too-wild animal lives (the dog house or the dog's bed). Locate something like the jungle hammock (a bed). Find where the native's clothes are kept (a closet). Go to where you relax after a safari (lounge chair). Find where a monkey lives (a tree).

Players will participate in pairs, so you'll need a set of the same clues for each pair (if you're having ten guests, make five sets). Use five different colors of balloons, one color for the clues of each pair. Thus, if you have six clues, you'll need six balloons in each color. With a marking pen, label each balloon set from one through six. Next assemble each set of clues in a different order so that players won't be able to follow one another from clue to clue. So you can hide the clues in a proper order, keep a list of the sequence in which the team with each color balloon will go. Doing one color of balloons at a time, roll up each clue and place well inside the neck of the balloon. Continue with each set of clues and a different color of balloon. You can do this in advance and wait until the party day to blow up all the balloons. While youngsters are playing the previous game in one room, use your list to place the balloons in the appropriate places—closet, dog bed, and so forth. For example, if clue number one in a set says: "Find where the natives keep their clothes" you will then place clue number two of that set in the closet. Retain the first balloon clue in each set to give when the game begins.

To start the game, divide the group into pairs, and give each pair the first balloon and remind them that they are *only to open balloons in their particular color.* At the word *Go* they are to start by breaking their first balloon and then trying to find the location of the second one. As they find the next place, they continue by breaking their color of balloon open, finding the next clue, and setting off again on the jungle treasure hunt. At the final destination, have a big collection of unwrapped treasures so that each guest can choose one.

4. **Creeping Through the Jungle** (twenty minutes). You'll need a rope and two yardsticks for this game that can be played on grass or carpet. (It's a quiet contrast to more active games that keep kids racing about.) Select one person to help you by holding the rope in one hand, and the yardstick upright in the other hand, as you hold the other end of the rope and the second yardstick. (This child will eventually get a turn by letting someone else hold the rope and yardstick.)

Kids line up and then crawl under the rope without touching it. If they touch the rope, they are out. Start with the rope at the three foot high point so that it's easy for everyone. Then lower it to two-and -one-half feet, two feet, eighteen inches, and then downward one inch at a time.

5. **"I'm Going on Safari and I'm Taking . . ."** (twenty minutes). This is a good going-home game since those leaving can easily drop out of this game. Guests sit in a circle and the verbal list is started with an item useful for a safari beginning with the letter A, then B, and so forth. For example, the first youngster might say, "I'm going on safari and I'm taking an arrow." The next one must repeat the line and add to it: "I'm going on safari and I'm taking an arrow and a bandage." The next line could be: "I'm going on safari and I'm taking an arrow, a bandage, and a camera."

6. **Lunch Safari** (ten minutes for the safari plus twenty minutes for eating. Cake and ice cream, and gift opening will take an additional thirty minutes.) Hide the lunches in trees, under bushes, in a wheelbarrow, and so forth, then the kids go on safari to find them. But, they must crawl everywhere they go so as not to upset the wild animals. Provide a tent or blanket at the lunch location.

FOOD: Pack the lunches in army surplus backpacks (one parent found them at a surplus store for a dollar each). Include a roasted and foil-wrapped chicken leg, a buttered roll, a banana in case they meet a monkey, a bag of peanuts for an elephant, a packet of animal crackers or trail mix, a canteen of jungle juice (canteens are also cheap at surplus stores or buy the inexpensive plastic kind). Serve ice cream and cake later.

    Tiger Cake: Make the cake, using a yellow cake mix, in one large round (the tiger's face) and two cupcakes (his ears). Use a bright-colored orange frosting. Then with a chocolate decorating tube, make eyes, nose, mouth, and whiskers. You can use flat chocolate mint patties on the ears, colored candies in the eyes, and candy corn for the teeth.

PRIZES/FAVORS: A visit to the surplus store will help you locate treasures for the end of the safari treasure hunt, and some take-home prizes such as compasses and folding utensils. You can also use animal stickers, small stuffed or wind-up animals, and small off-road vehicle toys.

PLANNING AHEAD: With your youngster, make a visit to a surplus store and buy backpacks and other prizes. You will need to shop elsewhere for balloons and some favors. For the games, make the elephant's trunk and the lion's tail and get the rope and two yardsticks. The jungle treasure hunt clues can be prepared ahead and then put in balloons to be blown up the day of the party. The food is simple to prepare on party day, but the cake can be made ahead and even frozen.

2. *The Olympics Party*

GUESTS: This party is tailored for grade-school youngsters, but can be adapted for teens by making the athletic events more difficult. Ten to fifteen guests are ideal.

THEME: Olympic events are frequently in the news since there are summer or winter games every other year. Everyone likes to be a winner, and at this party each guest will be.

LENGTH OF PARTY: About three hours (shorter for younger kids, longer for teens).

INVITATION: Using a drinking glass to trace around, draw the intertwined rings of the Olympic symbol on the face of the invitation. Inside, be sure to specify that guests wear sports clothes such as sweat suits or shorts and tank tops, and running shoes.

DECOR: Flags and banners will make the party area look festive. See if you can borrow flags of other nations. If not, use colorful streamers or help your child look in the encyclopedia in order to draw some flags. Have recorded music, such as the theme from "Rocky," or borrow a recording of national anthems from the library. Using bricks and boards, prepare the awards platform with the gold medal winner's place in the center, and the silver and bronze on left and right and slightly lower. Decorate it with crepe paper.

ACTIVITIES/GAMES: Have first, second, and third prizes ready for some of the contests. Make gold, silver, and bronze Olympic medallions following the instructions given below. You'll also need a whistle to start some of the races.

1. **The Icebreaker: Bucking Bronco Ball** (twenty minutes). This game requires a stopwatch and one of the large tough balls with a built-in handle, often called Bouncy Balls. (If you don't own one, it will be a valuable addition to your outdoor equipment, and it can also be used indoors in a large room.) Show how to sit on the ball, holding the handle, and bounce around as on a bronco. Make a start and a finish line and let youngsters practice as they arrive. When almost everyone is present, blow the whistle and use the stopwatch to see who can bounce the fastest from start to finish without falling over or off. Award three medallion prizes for first, second, and third place.

2. **The Ten-Yard Dash** (twenty minutes). Anyone can run thirty feet—but try it *backward!* On grass or carpet, make a course about thirty feet long with string for the starting and finish lines. Let participants run two at a time, then let the winners run for the semi-finals, and then have the finalists run. Award three medallion prizes for first, second, and third. Let those eliminated serve as cheerleaders.

3. **The Potato Relay Race** (twenty minutes). Divide the Olympians into two teams. Team members line up behind one another at the starting line. At the opposite end of the field should be a chair (if indoors) or tree (if outdoors). Two potatoes and two tablespoons are placed on the starting line. At the whistle, the first member of each team picks up the potato with the spoon and races around the chair or tree and back to the starting line where he puts the spoon and potato back on the line. The second team member then picks up the potato with the spoon and the relay continues. Have a simple prize, such as a plastic whistle on a string, for each member of the winning team to wear.

4. **Good Sports** (twenty minutes). Make each guest a sign (about five inches by seven inches in size) that ties in with Olympic competitions. These could be: downhill skier, figure skater, long distance runner, swimmer, diver, sprinter, high jumper, bob-sledder, pole vaulter, shot putter, discus thrower, cycler, sailor, equestrian, wrestler, boxer, or member of a volleyball, basketball, soccer, or ice hockey team. Tie a string on each sign so that a youngster can wear it around her neck but on her back. The group is seated in a circle and the host is the first "it," seated in the center with a list of the sports. "It" calls out the names of two different sports. The two with those signs must get up and exchange places with each other. At the same time, "it" tries to reach one of their places first. Whoever loses out on getting a place to sit must go to the center of the circle as the "it" and the game starts again as he calls the names of two other sports.

5. **Super Marksmanship** (twenty minutes). Save up eight empty cans (from juice, soup, fruit); remove the labels and wash. On a table (indoors or out), place cans singly and in groups about eight inches apart: a single can, then two cans with a third on top, a single can, then two cans on top of each other, then a single can. The object is to use three tennis balls to knock over as many cans as possible. Depending on the age of the participants, make a line about ten feet from the table (closer for younger guests). Select several youngsters to fetch thrown balls and reset the cans. A scorekeeper tallies how many cans fall over and each player gets a score from zero to eight. After everyone has had a turn, let the top three play for the first, second, and third place medallions.

6. **Olympic Obstacle Course** (twenty minutes or more). This is a good last game before guests go home since youngsters like to play it over and over. Play it once, timing participants with a stopwatch, and awarding medallion prizes for the three fastest guests. Then let the kids play it as many times as they wish to better their scores. Create the obstacle course in the yard (or in the family room): a large box to crawl through, an ottoman or bench to climb over, a bike tire or hula hoop to put over the head and then step out of, a rope to climb, a two-step ladder to climb and jump from, a series of pieces of construction paper to hop on, a card table to crawl under, and finally a series of three boxes taped together to crawl through. For younger children you may want to lay a string from one obstacle to the next to keep them on course.

(Food, cake eating, and gift opening will add about forty-five minutes to this party.)

FOOD: Have a truly international buffet with easy-to-make items associated with various countries. Here is a sample menu, but you can come up with your own tasty choices. Chinese egg rolls or wonton (available frozen or from a Chinese restaurant), Swedish meatballs on toothpicks, French crepes filled with chicken salad, Polynesian fruits (mango, pineapple, banana) served in papaya shells, Swiss hot chocolate or American soda pop, German chocolate cake. You may want to put signs by each item so kids know what country the food represents.

PRIZES/FAVORS: Make Olympic awards from red/white/blue ribbon and medallions made in gold, silver, and bronze. For the gold ones, you could purchase large chocolate coins covered in gold foil or cover another candy with gold foil. For the silver ones, cover large mint patties with silver foil. And to make the bronze ones, cut a circle of yellow paper the size of the mint patty and place on top of the candy. Then cover with pink plastic wrap to give it the bronze look. Affix the medallions with glue and staples to the wide ribbon so that they can be hung around each winner's neck. Provide a table, with cards showing the names of the Olympic players, where the already-won medallions can be placed during the strenuous games. For the games suggested above, you'll need twelve medallions plus some special awards to be used in case a youngster doesn't win any of the regular medallions. These special awards are medallions made from a plastic wrapped mint and labeled "Winner."

In a large silver bowl, put wrapped take-home gifts with a sports theme—small items such as water goggles, puzzles, balls, yo-yos—all easily found at a variety store.

PLANNING AHEAD: This party requires advance preparations, but they can be done well ahead with the help of your youngster. Prepare invitations and flags or banners. Obtain the bucking bronco ball. Prepare for the games and make the medallion awards. Make the cake ahead and freeze it. Final food preparations can be accomplished the day of the party.

3. Clown College

GUESTS: Invite up to a dozen uninhibited grade-schoolers.

THEME: Clown antics, silly jokes, and fun under your own big top.

LENGTH OF PARTY: Three hours. However, one hostess planned a one-hour party at the house followed by a trip to a local circus. You could also stay home, but have a clown come and entertain for thirty minutes, showing party-goers how to do clown tricks. However, these two options are not required to have fun at Clown College.

INVITATION: Invite guests via balloon. Purchase the longer narrow ones, inflate them (not completely), and tie a string bow to hold them shut. With a permanent marking pen, letter onto the balloons the pertinent information: date, time, place, occasion, RSVP number. Then deflate the balloons and send in envelopes to the guests.

DECOR: Lots of balloons and crepe paper streamers in bright colors are all you need.

ACTIVITIES/GAMES:

1. **The Icebreaker: Be a Clown!** (twenty minutes). As guests arrive, let them choose from a dress-up box of Clown College clothes (which you've collected from garage sales). Have baggy pants, big shorts and shirts in bright colors, belts, as well as big gloves and shoes, suspenders, bow ties, glasses, bandanas, and even wigs!

2. **Face-painting and Hat-making** (thirty minutes). These activities go on simultaneously. One adult watches over the hat-making table as another paints the face of each clown. (Practice in advance so you can quickly do the exaggerated big mouth with corners turned up or down, big arched eyebrows, a tear below one eye, rosy cheeks, frown lines, etc.)

For the hat-making, have a work area with paint, marking pens, glue, elastic cord, and large foam or plastic bowls (the size used for cereal). First, each guest glues two bowls together *bottom-to-bottom.* Then with poster paint or markers, and glitter and stickers, the clown decorates the bowls. Finally, an elastic cord is stapled from side to side as a chin strap so that the hat stays on.

3. **Clown Identification Cards** (fifteen minutes). So that they can enter Clown College, novice clowns need ID cards. With a Polaroid camera, take a photo of each clown in some ridiculous pose (doing a headstand, jumping in the air, making a face, bent over with back to the camera looking between her legs, and so forth). Clowns mount the photos on cardboard and letter on their clown name (Chuckles, Pookie, Big Mouth, Silly Susie, Henry Hobo, Bumper, etc.). Then with a paper punch and length of ribbon, each clown completes the ID card and hangs it around her neck.

4. **Pushin' Peanuts** (fifteen minutes). Circus clowns love peanuts! For this game you'll need an unshelled peanut and a toothpick for each player. Put string on the carpet or grass to make a starting line and a finish line—about fifteen feet apart. The object is to get the peanut from the starting line to the finish line by pushing it with the toothpick. It is not to be hit but rather pushed, and this isn't as easy as it sounds. Divide the clowns into groups of three or four. The clowns in one group race at the same time to determine a winner. When all groups have determined a winner, these race against each other. Award peanut butter/chocolate candy prizes for the winners.

5. **The High-Wire Act** (fifteen minutes). Place one two-by-four piece of lumber, about eight feet in length, between two lifts so that it is only about twelve inches off the carpet or grass. (For safety, move furniture or other hazards away from the "high wire.") With a broom handle or an umbrella for balance, let each clown practice walking the high wire. To make it easier, have clowns remove their shoes. To make it

harder, use a blindfold. Let everyone practice, then have the competition with prizes for those who make it from one end to the other with eyes open, and then blindfolded.

6. **Crazy Clown Catches** (twenty minutes). Remember those bowl hats? Well, they have a purpose besides keeping clown heads warm. In advance, make many three-inch-square beanbags. The object is for a clown to toss them into his own bowl hat, the toss being made no higher than shoulder height. Give everyone time to practice, then have the competition to see how many catches a clown can make in one minute. Award prizes for the top scores.

7. **The "Ballooney" Sandwich.** This is a good competition to play as guests are leaving for home. You'll need a start and finish line and a number of large balloons. Clowns pair off and make a ballooney sandwich by standing back-to-back with a balloon between them. They must keep the balloon off the floor, not using their hands or holding hands, as they shuffle their way from the start to the finish line. Dropping or popping the balloons means they have to start over. Give prizes for those reaching the finish line first. (Gift-opening and eating will add about forty-five minutes to this party.)

FOOD: Peanuts and popcorn are must snacks before the lunch or supper. And don't try to be original with this menu; it has to be hot dogs (with toppings of cheese, chili, onions, mustard, and ketchup), fries or chips, and lemonade. If it's summertime, include watermelon slices.

For dessert, serve clown cones. Melt chocolate bars in the microwave and paint the chocolate onto pointed ice-cream cones. Make about three at a time and let them cool. Next, put round balls of ice cream on a wax paper-covered cookie sheet. Using aerosol whipped cream, make a frilly collar around the ice cream ball and press jelly beans into the collar. Press the cone hat in place. Add coconut hair, candy eyes, cherry nose, and an orange segment mouth. Freeze until very hard. Just before serving, remove from the wax paper and place on colorful paper plates.

PRIZES/FAVORS: Each guest gets to take home an official-looking diploma shown on the next page. Stationery stores often have blank certificates that you can use or you can create them on the computer or copy the one on the the following page.

Prizes for the various competitions should tie in with the clown theme: noisemakers, fake noses, false teeth or eyebrows, popcorn balls, candy, stickers, magic tricks.

PLANNING AHEAD: If you plan to go to a circus or import a clown, arranging these will be your first task. Then send the invitations. After that, visit a magic shop or

This is to certify that

_____
(clown's name)

has graduated from CLOWN COLLEGE

on _____
(date)

with excellence in _____
(specialty)

certified by _____
(party giver's name)

From *The Family Party Book*, copyright © 1996 by Caryl Krueger

party store to get ideas for decorations and favors. Collect the clown clothes, prepare the games and activities, practice face painting, and make and freeze the clown cones. The remainder of the food is easy!

4. The TV Party

GUESTS: Kids nine through twelve like this party, which works well with up to a dozen youngsters.

THEME: Everything to do with the small screen—comedies, dramas, game shows, cartoons, actors and actresses—maybe even the Simpsons will come! (You're going to record it all with a video camera for replay at the end of the party.)

LENGTH OF PARTY: Three to four hours.

INVITATION: Make an invitation that looks like a ticket. You can do this on computer or by printing carefully. Cut colored paper the size of a business envelope. On one side print in large letters: Admit One—Priority Seating. On the other side: You're invited to the taping of the (party-giver's name) Show! Meet the stars, be on the set, be famous! (Then give the date, time, place, and dress.)

DECOR: Decorate your party room with silver stars hung from the ceiling. Place video posters on the walls (you can get these from your video rental store since they throw away outdated ones).

ACTIVITIES/GAMES:

1. **The Icebreaker: Be a Star!** (twenty minutes). Almost everyone has seen the handprints of the stars in cement. Using old cardboard boxes (one per guest), cut down the sides so that the boxes are about three inches deep. Line up the boxes on the floor or patio (covered with newspaper), on the grass, or at the entry. Have a large spotlight to make this activity look important. Get bags of ready-mix quick-setting cement and prepare it according to the instructions so that it is still wet when the party begins. Make it about two inches deep.

Then, as guests arrive, they will make a handprint and sign their name for posterity. (Have paper towels to clean off hands.) These boxes of cement will set up sufficiently so that they can be taken home by the guests at the end of the party.

2. **Dress Rehearsal** (twenty minutes). Attach a sign with a star's name to the *back* of each guest (let your own youngster select TV stars that are currently best-known among his friends). Give everyone cheap sunglasses to wear (to disguise them from their bothersome fans). They can then mingle, eat TV snack foods such as popcorn and Cracker Jack, and ask yes/no questions about themselves in hopes of guessing who they are. When a star has guessed his identity, he takes the sign off his back, puts it on his front, and tries to act like that star. Have the video camera running during this game, and when all of the stars have identified themselves, play back the video for all to see.

3. **Showtime** (sixty minutes or more depending on the size of the party). Divide

the guests into groups of two or three. They are now going to create a television program of their own. Let them meet in various parts of the house to devise the plan for a three-to-five minute production. Tell them that you will help with props and even suggest ideas if they're stuck. Some ideas are: The Cooking Show (supply a chef's hat, cooking materials), The Talk Show (a desk for the host and a chair for the guest), The Sports Interview (a sports helmet for the player and a fake microphone for the interviewer), The Drama Show, The Comedy Hour, The Quiz Show, a show from outer space, a commercial or infomercial—whatever they choose.

Guests can write a script outline or just ad lib for their few minutes on camera. In advance, you may want to create a "sound stage" with some bright lights aimed at the actors. Record each show on video, being sure to get close-ups. Let your youngster be the announcer to introduce each production and to hold up the applause sign at appropriate moments during the program.

4. **The Competition** (thirty minutes). To end the party, play back the complete video, then run a professional video—the choice of the guest of honor. Rent a funny Gallagher show, or part of a sci-fi or Steve Martin movie. (Gift opening and supper will add an hour to this party.)

FOOD: Make the meal a true dining experience that TV stars would expect. It should be a sit-down banquet with candlelight, soft music, nice china, and linens. Two adults, dressed as waiter/waitress, should serve. The menu might include: a salad course with rolls, quiche or pasta with fruit compote, sparkling cider, and a baked Alaska (an impressive but easy-to-make dessert found in most cookbooks).

PRIZES/FAVORS: Of course you hope the stars will take home their cement slab! And they already have their star sunglasses. At the dinner, the guest of honor should present the traditional Emmy Awards for all of the shows—funniest, weirdest, most dramatic, and so forth. These awards can be television magazines, a coupon good for a video rental, a large bag of popcorn, or actual little trophies that you can find at party stores.

PLANNING AHEAD: The invitations, decorations, and game preparations can be done well in advance (everything except mixing the cement). The video can be rented the day before. Also, the adult in charge of the video camera should check the equipment and do a practice run to see how the lighting and sound will work. The food is a bit more involved than some parties, but it can be made in about two hours the day of the party.

5. *Old MacDonald's Party*

GUESTS: This party is for youngsters ages nine through twelve, but can be adapted for younger children. Ten to twelve guests are ideal. Suggest overalls, jeans, plaid shirts, gingham dresses or shirts, and boots or lace-up shoes that are comfortable for the hayride, dancing, and games.

THEME: Loosely based on farm life, this party provides opportunities for preteens to socialize with the opposite sex in a casual environment.

LENGTH OF PARTY: Three to four hours, depending on activities.

DECOR: Hold this party at a barn, park, or in the family room at home. Provide bales of hay for sitting on (give them to a horse owner afterwards), lantern lighting (not candles), and red-checked fabric or paper for tablecloths and napkins.

ACTIVITIES/GAMES:

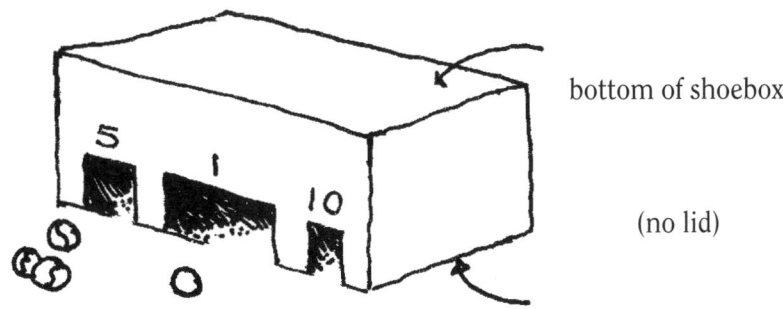

bottom of shoebox

(no lid)

1. **The Icebreaker: Put the Horse in the Barn** (twenty minutes). Prepare three shoe boxes in this way: cut three square openings along the upper edge of the box on one of the long sides. Make the openings in three sizes, the largest labeled "1," the midsize labeled "5," and the smallest labeled "10." These boxes, turned upside down on the floor, are three barns with stalls. Provide marbles to represent horses. The guests sit on the floor at a start line and are given five marbles to roll toward the nine openings. One person keeps score and the highest total gets a prize.

2. **The Hayride** (sixty minutes). For safety, most hayrides are now held on private property away from busy roads. Some farms will provide a hayrack for use on their property, and some park districts permit hayrides. Depending on local laws, flatbed trucks with hay in them can be used on back roads. Make one rule: Hayriders must remain seated. Encourage conversation, storytelling, and singing.

3. **How Many Beans Will Farmer MacDonald Plant?** (ten minutes). When youngsters return from the hayride, they will be hungry! As the food is being set out, have a guessing time. In advance, fill a jar with beans and be sure to count them (time-consuming but necessary). Let kids guess how many beans are in the jar. The nearest correct answer wins the prize: the jar of beans!

4. **The Chicken Coop** (fifteen minutes). After eating, explain that Farmer MacDonald's chicken eggs have rolled out of the chicken coop and that it's important to get them back as soon as possible. In advance, prepare four empty egg shells by making a small hole in each end and blowing out the contents into a bowl (save for making scrambled eggs). You can color the eggs if you wish. Have a start line and a finish line (the chicken coop), which can be just a line of hay on the floor.

Divide the players into four teams for the relay race and place an egg on the starting line for each team. Give the first team member a piece of cardboard about eight-by-ten inches in size. The object is to "fan" the egg to the finish line and back using the cardboard, but not touching the egg with it. Prizes for the winning team can be candy eggs.

5. **Square Dancing** (thirty-to-sixty minutes). With the aid of recorded music, introduce country dancing. (Most libraries will have both the music and the simple instructions.) "The Virginia Reel" and "Turkey in the Straw" are good dances for beginners. Youngsters this age also enjoy simple line dances. (Supper and gift opening will add at least an hour to this party.)

FOOD: Country-style food served in a basket can be fried chicken, potato wedges, deviled eggs, melon slices, and lemonade. Dips and veggies can be served earlier in the party. For dessert, try the Texas sheet cake, described at the end of this chapter, which provides a lot of surface for decorating as a birthday cake or with small plastic farm animals.

PRIZES/FAVORS: Game prizes can be animal soundmakers purchased at a party store. For take-home favors, let your youngster help make tote bags out of old jeans and fill them with pencils, tablets, trail mix, magazines, POGS, oatmeal cookies, puzzles, and so forth.

PLANNING AHEAD: Before sending the invitations, be sure to make arrangements for the hayride and the location for the party. Obtain recordings of the country dance music. To make the tote bags, use old jeans or buy similar material from a fabric store. The three games require a minimum of preparation and the foods are hearty and simple. The cake freezes well and can be made ahead.

SIX MORE PARTY THEMES

1. **The Wake-Up Party.** Girls like this variation on the all-night slumber event. Invite the guests for a 7:00 A.M. to 11:00 A.M. party. They come in their PJs, carrying their pillows. Pancakes with sausage and juice are served on trays in the bedroom or party room. And, of course, there should be a rich and gooey coffee cake served at midmorning! Activities include the usual pillow fights and a pajama fashion show. The best activity is pillowcase decorating, using white pillowcases and indelible marking pens. After each guest has decorated a pillow case, the girls like to write messages and sign one another's cases, which become mementos of this party.

2. **Wild West Shoot-Out.** The seven-to-ten-year-old set enjoys a party with lots of excitement. Encourage cowboy dress. Play the game "Laughing Cowboy." On the grass or carpet, kids lie down in a large circle, each one resting his head on the previous youngster's tummy. When every youngster has a head on his tummy, the guest of honor shouts a hearty "Ha!" The one whose head is on that child's tummy must say "Ha, Ha!" and so it goes, each one adding a "Ha!" When you can't stand any more laughing, it's time for games of cowboy skill: lassoing a chair, rounding up wild

horses (tag), knocking cans off a fence (using balls), and eating grub around the campfire.

3. **The Penguin Party.** Pool parties are always fun in warm weather. Encourage kids to bring swim fins for speedy swimming in races, keep-away, and Marco Polo. Also, have a relay by dividing the group into two teams, each lined up along a different side of the pool. With a rubber ducky for each team and a Ping-Pong paddle that is passed from one team member to the next, the team members push their ducky from one end to the other. When it's time to eat, two penguins (adults wearing fins and simulated tuxes) can serve fish tacos or fish sticks with fries.

4. **Field Trip Parties.** Sometimes a party given away from home is especially effective. Alternate party locations, in addition to a park or beach, are: skating rink, horseback-riding stable, ball game, miniature golf, circus, a suitable movie, arboretum, observatory, zoo, haunted house, cowboy museum, train museum, or other local attraction. For older grade-schoolers, a party on a houseboat is quite special.

5. **Hobo Party.** Tattered clothes are in style at this party that begins with the making of Junque Chapeaus. At yard sales, buy derbies and bonnets for kids to redesign as their own hobo hats by attaching various junk items: old kitchen tools, broken toys, fake flowers, odd pieces of jewelry, and so forth. Then in pairs, they're off on a scavenger hunt two-by-two in the neighborhood (adult supervision recommended). Items to collect include: white button, candle, small mirror, postcard, thimble, lollypop, shoe, 1992 penny, emery board, plaid ribbon, old key, flashlight battery, eraser, pink soap, shoehorn, baby photo, gum, sock, shoelace. Back at the house, there can be hobo meals served in bandanas affixed to sticks. Plan a hobo relay race with participants racing to put on old clothes (big overalls, sweater, and boots), run to the finish line, take them off, and bring them back to the start line for the next runner. An alternate activity to the scavenger hunt, providing the party is held on a Saturday, is a visit to a swap meet or flea market where each guest is given one dollar and told to find the most unique buy. It's interesting to see what youngsters can bargain for!

6. **The Mall Party.** This party requires two adults and two teams of four to five youngsters. In advance, the adults have prepared clues that will take the teams all around the mall—always walking in a group with an adult. Each adult has the same set of clues, but they are given out in a different order. The adult knows each destination but does not give hints, merely acknowledging when the team has reached the correct destination. Clues might be: What Goes Up Must Come Down (escalator or elevator), The Know-It-All (information booth), Mall Blueprint (the directory board), Toys for Big Boys (men's equipment store), Lullaby Time (baby store), Where Elvis Lives (music store), and so forth. At midpoint, have a clue that says "Sweet Success" (the candy store) where you've paid in advance for a bag of candy for each player. The final clue should lead to the hamburger or ice cream shop where the group gathers to eat.

FIVE TESTED AND APPROVED GAMES

1. **What's on the Tray?** This game is still popular after decades of play. On a tray place twenty items: baby sock, computer disk, red pencil, paper clip, coaster, cracker, and so forth. Cover the tray with a cloth and place it in the center of the circle. Give players pencil and paper, and have them sit around the tray. Uncover the tray and let the group look (but not write) for one minute. Cover the tray and let them list what they saw. Give prizes for the highest totals.

2. **The Giant's Game.** Divide the group into teams of at least three, each team having a separate meeting place in the room. One team is called the Giant's Team and stands in the middle of the room. Together, they decide on something the Giant wants and then they announce in bellowing voices: The Giant wants . . . (a table, cat, TV, sofa, refrigerator, car, hamburger, piano, wastebasket, bathtub). The team members cooperate creatively to physically become that object. The Giant's team chooses the best representation and that team becomes the next Giant Team.

3. **Name Five.** This pencil-and-paper game requires participants to name five things in the same category, such as: lakes (i.e., Michigan, Superior, Tahoe, Salt, Geneva), planets, cities in Europe, mountain peaks, musical instruments beginning with T, countries in South America, birds and animals of Australia, computer commands, unlucky things to do, foods eaten with a spoon, and games played with a ball. The player with the most answers wins.

4. **Vegetable Animals.** Provide trays of vegetables: carrots, celery, radishes, squash, cauliflower, potatoes, sprouts, lettuce, and so forth, and dishes of toothpicks. Each participant is to make a person or animal by fitting the vegetables together with the toothpicks. Use of a knife, scissors, or peeler is permitted. The entries are displayed and the guests vote for the best. At one party, the winning entry was a clown with a radish head, alfalfa sprouts hair, a potato slice collar, a zucchini body, carrot arms and legs, and floppy lettuce shoes. Another charming entry was a tiny radish-faced baby wrapped in a lettuce leaf blanket.

5. **The Human Conveyor Belt.** Youngsters (at least eight) lie down on carpet or grass, close together side-by-side, face up. At the word *Go*, they turn together to the left, then face down, and back to face up, all the time remaining tight to the person next to them. Practice this until they can do it without separating from the youngsters next to them. Now, you are ready to load the conveyor with human cargo. With the conveyor belt tightly in place, one youngster lies down *across* the other bodies. Then, the kids begin to roll and you will see that the "cargo" moves along the belt until deposited at the other end. Let everyone have a chance to ride the conveyor belt.

FEEDING THE GANG

1. **Snappy Snacks.** Bag those old chip/dip recipes in favor of some new snacks. Try these: Celery logs: eight ounces of cream cheese mixed with a half cup of granola

and stuffed into celery stalks. Tex-Mex Popcorn: one half cup of melted margarine mixed with a half cup grated cheese and two tablespoons taco seasoning, tossed well with popped corn. Bacon sticks: crisp bread sticks rolled in grated cheese, wrapped in bacon, and microwaved for four minutes.

2. **Make Your Own Submarine.** Putting together a giant sandwich can be a great party event. Depending on the number of guests, buy several very long loaves of bread, sliced the long way, and line them up on a kitchen counter. Prepare fillings in advance and let each person be in charge of one layer: spreads such as mayonnaise and mustard, sliced meat, cheese, onions, pickles, tomatoes, lettuce, and so forth.

3. **Peek-a-boo Sandwiches.** Each peek-a-boo sandwich will require two pieces of bread. On the lower piece, spread a bright colored filling such as strawberry jam, ham salad, or grape jelly. On the upper piece, cut a design right through the bread: big eyes, a leering mouth, and so forth. If you wish, you can put spread on this bread, too: peanut butter, mayonnaise, and so forth. Next, firmly place the cut-out piece (spread side down) on top of the bottom slice. Make many different faces and arrange these see-through sandwiches on a platter to show off the faces.

4. **Crazy Cones and Cupcakes.** Confuse party-goers with these tricky treats that aren't what they seem to be. Buy waffle cones with flat bottoms. Prepare a cake mix and fill each one two-thirds full (you should be able to fill about twelve cones). Bake fifteen to twenty minutes on a cookie sheet at 350 degrees until the batter puffs up like a big scoop of ice cream. When cool, put frosting on top. (These can be frozen if made ahead.) For the "cupcakes," use sturdy foil muffin pan liners. Fill with ice cream and decorate with sprinkles on top so they look like cupcakes. Make these in advance and keep them frozen until serving time when you put one cupcake and one cone on each youngster's plate. See how soon they catch on to the hoax.

5. **Texas Sheet Cake.** This big cake is always a favorite:
Bring to a boil:
½ lb. margarine
4 tablespoons cocoa
½ cup shortening
1 cup water
Sift together:
2 cups flour
2 cups sugar
Put hot mixture over dry mixture and add, mixing well:
½ cup buttermilk
1 teaspoon baking soda
2 eggs
1 teaspoon vanilla
Pour into greased and floured nine-by-thirteen-inch pan.
Bake at 400 degrees for twenty to twenty-five minutes.

Five minutes before cake is done, mix and bring to a boil:
¼ pound margarine
4 tablespoons cocoa
6 tablespoons milk

Remove from heat and beat in a one pound box of powdered sugar, 1 cup chopped nuts (optional) and one-half teaspoon vanilla. Spread on cake immediately upon removing from oven.

For a spectacular cake, don't miss the Volcano Cake recipe at the end of chapter 3.

* * *

You may want to read the following chapter about teen parties. Some can be adapted for grade-school youngsters. Also, read chapters 7 and 8 for seasonal parties and special occasion parties.

Teen Extravaganzas

or teen parties, you can throw structure out the window! This doesn't mean that the party has no planned events, but it does mean that the people, not the plan, take the lead. So, giving a teen party is usually quite different from the more complete party organization required for younger kids.

What goes on at parties is highly important to the teens, but numerous surveys of their parents show deep concerns about those parties and whether they should allow their kids to attend all—or any.

A teen party should never become a three-D event: dates, drinks, and drugs. That's no party at all, but rather an invitation to disaster. For teen parties there should be a simple framework, and the four cornerposts of that framework are a good mix of guests, music and activities, conversation, and food—and lots of the last.

The parents of each guest (but especially the host's parents) cannot relinquish responsibility for what happens at a party. They *are* the people ultimately responsible, and for their own protection, and that of the guests, they need to know what's going on. Forget the notion that an adult chaperon means the party won't be fun. While these chaperons should not take part in the party, they must still be on the scene, in the background yet definitely aware and alert to party activities.

THE BASIC RULES FOR TEEN PARTIES

1. **A guest list.** Whether invitations are written or phoned, the parent has the legal, ethical, and practical right to know *in advance* who's coming. And that means a written guest list.
2. **No gate crashers.** If the party is inside the house, keep the doors locked and open

them only to admit guests. If your teen didn't extend an invitation to a person, that person is not welcome.

3. **No drifting.** Guests are not to come to a party, leave, and return again unless they tell some very important reason before leaving. Drifting in and out of a party usually means that the guest is going out to get or use drugs or alcohol. So, when a guest leaves, there's no return privilege.

4. **Chaperons.** Until all the youngsters are of legal age, parties need at least two chaperons. The parents may want to invite another person or couple to spend the evening watching television or playing cards in another part of the house. Going to the kitchen for food or offering help in an activity gives the adults the opportunity to quietly move on the fringes of the party scene and be aware of what is happening. Let it be known that parties at your house *always* have a chaperon. And when your youngster goes to a party at another house, call to ask who will be on hand as a chaperon. If you love and care about their safety, you will routinely and matter-of-factly make this call. And you will *never* permit your child to attend an unchaperoned event.

5. **No beer barrels.** Providing beer for kids is not cute. There are plenty of special drinks that are nonalcoholic (see the end of this chapter for one delicious beverage recipe). If teens need alcohol to enjoy a party, there is something wrong with the kids and with the party. I hope that you're already aware that you are legally responsible for the actions of youngsters who drink alcohol or use illegal drugs at your house—both during and after the party. See that they don't. If somehow they do, call their parents to come and drive them home.

6. **No closed doors.** Other than the locked entry doors, all other doors should be wide open (except when a bathroom is in use). Even though bedrooms are not party rooms, the doors are open and remain open. The only door allowed to be closed is that of another family member who is not part of the party.

7. **No dark rooms.** While there may be a game that is played in the dark, generally the party needs some light. The lights can be low for talking and dancing, but the lights are not to be switched off.

8. **Ending time.** While guests of this age may arrive on time or, more usually, late, the ending time of the party should be firmly enforced. See that this time is put in the invitation and make sure that the kids drive or are driven home at the announced hour.

9. **Having fun.** Don't be fooled into thinking that teens don't enjoy fun—even silly fun. Most teens are far less sophisticated than you are led to believe. There is a vast difference between the interests of thirteen-year-olds and nineteen-year-olds—although sometimes the thirteen-year-olds are the more mature!

10. **Planning ahead.** Don't let a party just develop—make a plan with your teen. You may decide during the party to drop part of the plan, but at least be prepared with one.

* * *

Now this set of rules could be discouraging to a teen with a warped sense of what is fun; but he should agree to these rules and understand the four cornerposts of the party (good guests, music and activities, conversation, food) and not depend on the crutches of alcohol or drugs.

So let's now consider those four cornerposts and then some simple themes that will make the party memorable fun.

GUESTS

Depending on the size of your home, plan a party for twelve to twenty-four guests. The teen giving the party will have definite ideas on who to include, but you should encourage a diversified group—good friends, new friends, extroverts, introverts—so that the party isn't just a cliquish event for the in-group of everyday buddies.

Youngsters at this age like to feel in charge of their parties. In order to make this happen, and happen smoothly, parents need to suggest and discuss a time schedule plus a duty schedule that includes guests. Among those invited, there should be some close friends willing to help with greeting, food, games, and other party elements. It will be a better party if the parent does less and the kids do more.

MUSIC AND ACTIVITIES

Whether or not there will be dancing, music is usually an essential. If it's background music, try to choose instrumental selections. Nonvocal music doesn't conflict with conversation or games.

For dancing, vocal music will usually be most popular. Parents should exercise some control of the verbal content of this music in order to avoid selections with messages that are contrary to their family values. With so much music to choose from, you should be able to find recordings that don't promote violence and promiscuity. If recordings are to be borrowed, check those out ahead of time.

Because dancing can be very important to older teens, see that the music is selected in advance and make sure the player and speakers are working properly.

If the party is to have a DJ, talk with him or her when making the arrangements in order to decide the type of music that is wanted, in keeping with your family values. Make arrangements to roll up carpets and move furniture on patios or decks, so that there is an adequate dance floor.

It's a courtesy to neighbors to let them know in advance when there will be a party with music, and that the music will stop at midnight.

Today there is a renewed interest in games for teens, and these can add a lot of fun to a party. You'll find many tested suggestions in this chapter. Games bring the group together and provide healthy competition and opportunities for good humor.

CONVERSATION

Younger teens are more apt to be interested in playing games and organized activities; older teens can be very content with opportunities to talk, dance, and enjoy music. Conversation flows easily when guests are comfortable with each other and with the setting.

To provide a party environment conducive to conversation, you need cozy places to sit such as a group of comfortable chairs, adjacent sofas, or cushions on the floor. Background music and low lighting lead to longer conversations with greater depth and exploration of mutual interests.

Don't overlook the possibility of having an icebreaker activity that gives teens some camaraderie with other guests. You'll find some further game ideas at the end of this chapter.

FOOD

Everything else can be perfect, but if the food isn't great, the party won't be a success. Most parties require sodas and snacks and then the main eating event followed by something sweet. It's so easy to serve hamburgers and ice cream, but it isn't much more work to have an inventive menu, one that can even involve the guests in its preparation.

Provide flat surfaces on which to eat and coasters for the beverages (so that your mementoes of the party do *not* include carpet and furniture stains). A clean garbage can with a liner can be used for the paper refuse, making cleanup easier.

But most important, have plenty of food on hand. With teens, there will be little wasted! See the section "Let's eat!" in this chapter for innovative ideas.

THEMES FOR TEENS

While clowns and finger painting are too childish, a simple theme for a party is still acceptable. Some of the parties and games described in this chapter are for kids as young as thirteen, but there are also ideas for college-age teens. Here are some teen-tested favorites:

1. *The Karaoke Party*

Everyone secretly longs to be a star! A karaoke party lets singers pretend to be performing with bands and groups. If you can't borrow the karaoke equipment, you can rent it. In advance, consult with the teens as to their favorite musicians and obtain the music and song sheets for these songs. Videotaping the karaoke performances makes an hilarious and memorable playback later in the party.

2. *The Pancake Party*

Pancakes are the focal point for both the fun and the food at this event, a special favorite of younger teens. In advance, make about a dozen pancakes and obtain two identical skillets. Divide the group in half for a pancake flipping relay:

Give each team captain the skillet with one pancake in it. (Have some spare pancakes ready should one get demolished.) Using the length of the partyroom, make an easy obstacle course: over a cushion, around a chair at the far end, over the cushion again and back to the start line. During this race, each person must flip the pancake into the air once on the way to the chair, and once on the way back to the start line. Dropping the pancake means you have to start over. The first team to complete the relay wins.

Next, have a pancake flipping contest, using a yardstick to measure who can flip a pancake the highest—and catch it again.

The final event is a pancake-eating contest. Get willing volunteers to stuff themselves and let the others be their cheerleaders.

Of course, the food will have to be pancakes and with a grand variety of toppings: berries and other fruits, nuts, different syrups, ice cream and yogurt, chocolate chips and whipped cream.

3. Antonio, the Super Chef

Antonio is a super chef from Sicily and everyone must do what Antonio dictates—or else! At this party, the guests can enjoy music and talk as they put together Antonio's most famous gourmet dish: Minestra. (You can adapt this party for eight to sixteen guests.)

For serving a group of sixteen, you will need:

> 4 large stalks of broccoli
> 2 medium onions
> 2 8-ounce cans of peeled tomatoes
> 2 pounds of lean ground beef
> 4 cups of water
> Salt and pepper
> 1½ pounds of pasta (shells, bows, or elbows)
> 4 tablespoons olive oil
> 2 loaves of crusty bread
> 2 cloves of garlic
> ½ pound butter
> Parmesan cheese

Place these items in a row on the kitchen counter along with two very large cooking pots and one large skillet, a large bowl, cooking spoons, garlic press, measuring spoons, aluminum foil, a colander, table settings (including large bowls, napkins, large and small spoons, ice-cream dishes), a tureen, a bread platter, pot holders, and a small pan for melting butter. To complete the meal, you'll also want spumoni ice cream in the freezer and white grape juice in the refrigerator.

Before the party, prepare these eight direction cards and fold them in half, sealing

them with tape so they can't be read in advance. Divide the group into pairs and let the host deliver one card to each pair. The pairs will go into the kitchen one at a time, open and read their card, and perform their gourmet duties. This is what the cards should say:

Card 1: Antonio has put you in charge of the broccoli. Wash, then peel the stems, and cut them into small pieces about an inch long. Cut the heads into spoon-size florets. Put all into the bowl.

Card 2: Antonio loves onions and has chosen you to dice the two onions. (Don't forget to peel off the dry skin first.) In the large skillet, lightly brown the ground beef and the onions in four tablespoons of olive oil. Drain this mixture and return it to the pan.

Card 3: Antonio wants you to work precisely: Add the prepared broccoli to the large pot. Then add the two cans of tomatoes, two tablespoons of salt, and one teaspoon of pepper. Cover this with four cups of water and bring to a boil, then immediately turn this pan to low. Fill the second large pot three-fourths full with water and turn on the burner to medium. Tell the couple with card #5 to wait twenty minutes before going to work.

Card 4: Antonio has easy work for the less-talented chefs. First, turn on the oven to 400 degrees. Melt butter in a small pan and, using the garlic press, add the garlic to the butter and stir. Slice the bread and dip one side in butter. Sprinkle with parmesan cheese. Reassemble the loaf and wrap it in foil. Place it in the oven.

Card 5: Antonio has chosen the most talented assistants for this important work. Turn up the heat on the pot filled with water. In the other pot, check the broccoli for doneness and turn up the heat if it isn't done. When tender, turn off the burner, drain the broccoli mixture, and add it to the beef/onion mixture. Place the pasta in the second pot and cook according to directions on the package. When the pasta is done, drain it in the colander.

Card 6: Antonio is getting hungry, so work quickly. Take the drained pasta and add it to the broccoli/beef/onion mixture. Taste and add salt if needed. The consistency should be like a thick soup. Turn on the heat to low.

Card 7: Antonio has given you this job because of your creative ways. Set the table with napkins, utensils, and the big bowls. (If a buffet, arrange these items on the serving counter.)

Card 8: Antonio has entrusted you with the finishing touches. Pour the white grape juice. Put the hot bread loaves on platters and the main dish in the tureen. Call everyone to dinner. After dinner, put scoops of spumoni in the small bowls and serve.

Since Antonio is Italian, you could show a "spaghetti Western" or other Italy-related video after the food is gone.

4. The Pep Party

This works best as an all-girl's event. The guests should wear tennis shoes, sweaters, and short full skirts, but don't tell them more. Contact a nearby college and arrange to have from three to six cheerleaders (dressed in their uniforms) come to the party. Offer to make a donation directly to the school or to a charity in the school's name.

Decorate with college banners and large hand-painted pep signs, and have pompons available. When the cheerleaders arrive, they are to give lessons to the guests, teaching them cheers, steps, gymnastics, and other pep squad talents.

When the cheerleading lesson is over, the group will be hungry for football game foods such as hot dogs, hamburgers, or pizza.

5. The Wild and Wet Party

Although a Penguin Party is described in the chapter for grade-school kids, this pool party is especially for teens. It almost takes care of itself since almost everyone has a favorite pool game. Add these to give it a new twist:

Typhoon! Divide the guests into teams of three. Provide each with a plastic toy boat. Each team stands together in the water at poolside behind their "yacht." Without touching their boat, they are to be a typhoon and blow it to the opposite side. First boat to hit the other side of the pool wins.

Sinking Ship. The group is divided into teams of two or three. A rubber (not inflatable) ball is called "the ship." To start the game, the ship is tossed into the air—and after that, it sinks. This means that the person who catches it must keep it underwater at all times, but can pass it underwater to a fellow team member. The other teams try to save the sinking ship by grabbing it or diving underwater to take it away.

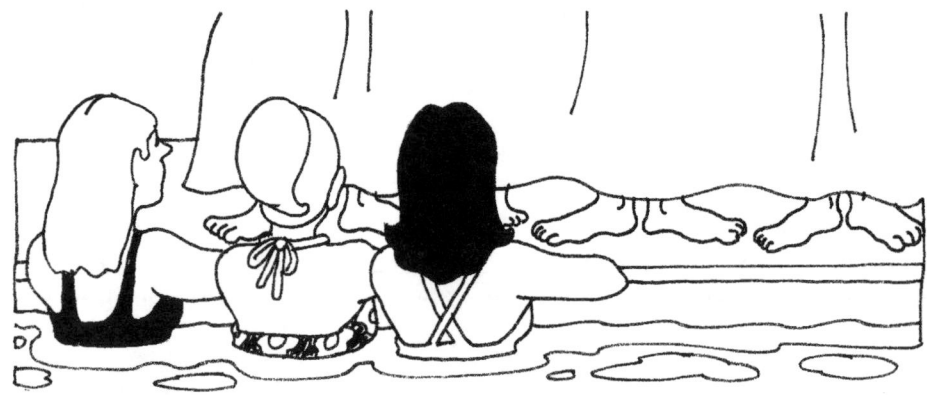

Sailor's Toes. This is for a party of couples. The girls stand in the pool with their backs to the pool edge as the boys get out and step behind a big sheet—or two—held so as to cover all but their feet. Then the girls turn around and study the feet, each one trying to find the feet of the fellow she came with. There will be big laughs as some feet get ignored and others are fought over.

Obstacle Course. Use some guests as human obstacles, the others as swimmers. Then switch. The object is to swim the watery course *without touching* any of the obstacles (if the human obstacle feels a touch, you're out of the game). The human obstacles each have a position: (1) In the shallow end, both feet on pool floor, one hand on pool edge. Swimmer must swim between obstacle and wall. (2) Hands and feet widely separated on pool wall. Swimmer must go between the hands and the feet. (3) Feet on pool floor, legs apart. Swimmer must go between legs. (4) Hands on pool edge at a corner, feet on pool wall. Swimmer must negotiate the corner. (5) In shallow water, with a hula hoop held underwater. Swimmer must swim through it. (6) With back to the wall and arms holding the edge, back arched. Swimmer must swim behind this obstacle and the wall.

Pool parties are especially successful for late afternoon and evening because it's enjoyable to swim in a lighted pool and then enjoy the refreshments by candlelight at small tables by the pool.

6. Sweet Sixteen Party

(For a guy, it can be called a Suave Sixteen Party.) A sixteenth birthday is a landmark, so make it special.

Adorable Babies. Ask guests to bring their own baby pictures. Pin these on a board and give everyone paper and pencil to guess who they are.

Birthday Suit. At a party shop or from a catalog, buy a "birthday suit" and some permanent marking pens (this will cost less than twenty dollars). This suit is a soft paper one-size-fits-all coverall that is worn by the guest of honor. Everyone enjoys drawing pictures, writing messages, and signing names right on the guest. (An alternate is a small T-shirt and mock diaper.)

Trike Relay. Borrow two tricycles and divide into teams for a relay race in the driveway. It may sound juvenile, but the teens love it!

Mime Time. Hire a mime to come and entertain, especially picking on the celebrant. You'll find mimes in the classified section of the phone book.

Food: For snacks, fill baby bottles with juice or soda, and have bowls of animal crackers. When it's time to eat, lay out a barbecue buffet. First, each guest takes a large piece of heavy-duty foil and places it on a plate. Then onto the foil goes all the fixings: bun, cheese, precooked barbecue meat, onions, olives, sauces. Near the end of the line, the package is bundled to make it air-tight, and labeled with the person's name. The bundle is then put on a pre-lit barbecue to cook for fifteen minutes, along with foil-wrapped corn on the cob. Serve salad on the plate while waiting for the bundles and the corn to cook.

7. *"Teacher Let the Monkeys Out" Party*

While graduation parties are popular for high school seniors, younger teens like to celebrate the end of the school year, too. This party is best when held the very day that classes end.

Intellectual games are in order, but these are the fun kind, and in some cases the wrong answer is as valued as the correct one. Use a big school bell to start the games and also to indicate when time is up.

School Art. Tell the group that they are going to draw pictures of their favorite school teacher. Give out crayons and paper—and then turn the lights out (or provide blindfolds if the room is too light). When the masterpieces are finished, the group can guess who the teachers are and vote on the best pictures, the artists receiving prizes.

Categories. It's a pencil and paper game you prepare in advance by listing twenty categories down the left side of a piece of paper (color, animal, bird, vegetable, fruit, automobile, mineral, food, profession, song, TV show, country, state, city, musician, item of apparel, book, flower, tree, movie). Make a copy for each person. At the party, select a letter (the host opens a book, shuts her eyes, and points to a letter). The group then has five minutes to write down something in each category that begins with the chosen letter, trying to select the most unique word. Grade the papers as a group, giving five points for an answer no one else has, three points if others have the same answer, and no points if no answer is given.

Dunce. Make a simple dunce cap for use in this game. First, each person writes out two questions they think might stump the group. (Spell *onomatopoeia*. What is the main ingredient in mayonnaise? What are the letters for the Roman numeral eighty-one? What is the capital of Illinois? How many blackbirds are there in the nursery rhyme? Who starred in the movie *Ace Ventura, Pet Detective*?) Put all the questions in a bowl, and let each person take turns drawing one and trying to answer. If he can't, he must wear the dunce cap until another person flunks a question.

Hidden Geography. Each person gets a copy of this game. Then, with pencil in hand, he must find the geographical locations buried in these sentences. (For younger teens, let them work in pairs.) Everyone gets the first one right.

1-River. Did you see the ma**n I le**ft behind at the corner?

2-River. He went somewhere with a messenger in an overcoat.

3-River. The gang established the headquarters in a garden and hid him there.

4-River. He always tried to please in every way although he hated my cooking.

5-River. I'm afraid he left because the ham is sour indeed.

6-Country. How can a damsel like me get him back?

7-Country. How much I let these kidnappers have depends on my funds and their demands.

8-Country. The terms being such, I naturally want to free him.

9-Country. If we agree, certainly I'll pay; if not, we fight!

10-Country. But my gun barrel is tiny in diameter.

11-City. I can hock the sterling, but will Anna polish it first?

12-City. Unfortunately, the sale might go awry and they'd not send him back to me.

13-City. Every kidnapper in the garden verified the exchange plan.

14-City. So I told Sara to gag the press and make the deal with them.

15-City. The meeting place was to be on Main St., Paul divulged.

16-State. Being vicious, they tried to model a war each time I stepped closer.

17-State. They even tried to color a dog purple to confuse us.

18-State. But the main event was the delicate negotiation for his release.

19-Continent. Was I a sucker to think they were reasonable!

20-Continent. When I asked if all liqueur operators were racketeers, they just gave up to the police, and we were reunited!

ANSWERS: 1: Nile, 2: Thames, 3: Ganges, 4: Seine, 5: Missouri, 6: Canada, 7: Chile, 8: China, 9: Greece, 10: India, 11: Anapolis, 12: Salem, 13: Denver, 14: Saratoga, 15: St. Paul, 16: Delaware, 17: Colorado, 18: Maine, 19: Asia, 20: Europe.

Bubble Blowers. Although teachers don't like gum-chewing, it's okay at this party, so provide tasty bubble gum and have a contest for the biggest bubble and the longest lasting bubble.

Serve food cafeteria-style on TV dinner plates you've saved. But don't serve cafeteria food!

8. The Backwards Progressive Dinner

This spreads the party preparations and activities over several houses (so no one family does all the work). It is most effective if the guests can be transported in one or two vans so that there can be fun between stops. At the first house the guests eat dessert. At the next house they get salad. Next comes the main dish, and finally appetizer snacks and punch. At each house the teen host chooses the music and a game or dancing.

9. The Couch Potato Party

This party offers more than just sitting and watching a big football game. Of course you'll need lots of comfy seating, at least two TV sets in different rooms, and a well-stocked buffet table. A hearty menu could be chili in a Crock-Pot to be served over baked potatoes (wrapped in foil and kept warm on a heating tray), coleslaw, and several kinds of cake with whipped cream. For continuous snacking, prepare bowls of popcorn with various flavors (plain, butter, cheese, cinnamon, caramel), and don't forget the soda pop.

To add interest to the game time, have guessing contests. Give each guest a supply of candy kisses. To enter a contest, they must give up a kiss. If they win with a correct guess or the nearest correct guess, they get all—or a share of—the kisses back. Three contests are announced at the start of each quarter. For the first quarter: the length of the opening kick, the number of turnovers, the score at the end of the quarter. For the second quarter: which team if any will score first, the number of fumbles, the score at the half. For the third quarter: the number of interceptions, how many passes will be completed, the score at the end of the quarter. For the fourth quarter: the number of sacks, the number of penalties, the final score.

MORE ACTIVITIES AND GAMES

If teens are to be involved and really enjoy games, the games have to be more interesting than passing an orange under the chin! Here are eight good suggestions.

1. **Outrageous Adjectives.** In advance, type up a fictitious story about the group attending. Leave blanks in the story (to be filled in later with adjectives—descriptive words) and include in the story the names of all those attending, leaving a space for an adjective before each name. For example, "Once upon a time there was a _____ group of teenagers who got together for a _____ party given by _____ Paul Jones. The funniest person at the party was _____ Sheila Smith."

At the party, the guests (who have no idea of the story) suggest outrageous adjectives while you fill in, as they are shouted out, in the order of the blanks. Encourage unusual and colorful adjectives. Then when all the blanks are filled in, read the story back for laughs.

2. **The Snapping Game.** Guests sit in a circle and number off, one through ____ (however many are playing). They must remember their own number since they are going to call and be called by number. Number one is the leader and starts the rhythmic clapping exactly as follows: Two hands slapped twice on legs, then two hands clapped together twice, then right hand snapped while saying his own number, then left hand snapped while saying the number of another person. Keeping the rhythm and without pause, this clapping/snapping sequence continues, but the person called now says *his* number on the right hand snap and another player's number on the left hand snap. If someone fails to respond or responds incorrectly, the game stops, the loser moves to the last place in the circle, takes that number, and all others move up and take the next higher number. Then, number one starts again. Number one can also control the pace of the game, starting slowly and then when most have got the idea, speeding up.

3. **Scavenger Hunts.** These can be great fun right within the party room, or out in a safe neighborhood. A hunt is a good icebreaker.

For an in-home hunt, secretly give each guest one item (whistle, handkerchief, sunglasses, red sock, ticket stub, dime, candy, photo, purple pen, silver ring, and so forth). These items are hidden on the person and never shown. Guests are given a list of these items and must go to each guest and ask just one question: "Do you have the whistle?" If so, they put the person's name on the list opposite that item. They may not ask the same person two questions in a row, but must go on to someone else to question and be questioned. By process of elimination, the questioning gets much easier and faster and the game ends with a winner who has found the owner of each item.

For an outdoor hunt, divide the group in pairs and give each a bag. Assign each pair to one side of nearby streets (so as not to totally pester the same neighbors many times). The list should have ten items such as: thimble, 1986 penny, purple crayon, plastic paper clip, pink ribbon, mint, baby diaper, a black hair taped on paper autographed by the owner, a newspaper from last week, a magazine picture of a car, a piece of dry dog food. Encourage players to be very polite. Make a thirty-minute time limit for all to return. The pair who finds the most items and returns first will be the winners.

4. **The String Maze.** This game can be used to find a partner for another game or for dancing, or to lead players to prizes. You will need to set it up in one room before the party (and remove any breakable items in the room).

Using a large ball of string, lay one string from the doorway, under and around furniture to a hidden prize. Do the same thing again, starting at the doorway going a different direction but crossing the first string, and leading to a prize. Continue weaving new strings until you have one for each player with all the loose ends at the

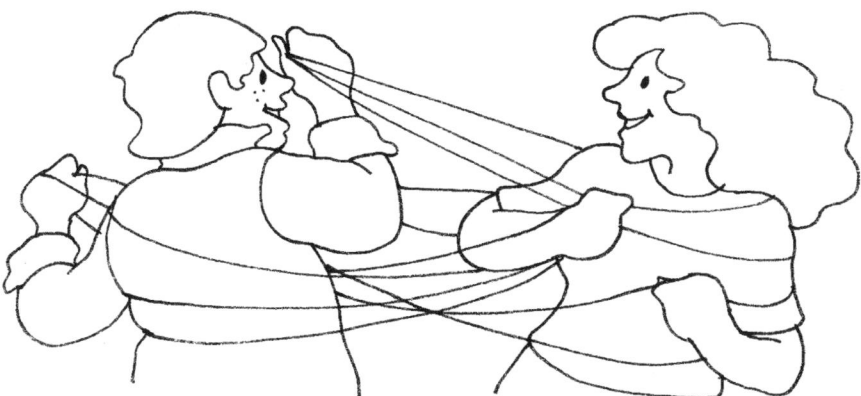

door. To play the game, the group gathers at the room door where each is given a string and told that she may not let go of it under any circumstances. However, she must carefully wind up the string and find the prize at the end. There will be lots of climbing under and over strings, a lot of laughing, and a few arguments over who is making a hopeless knot!

To play the game in order to locate a partner, do not put prizes at the ends of the strings, but rather start a person on each end of the string. In this way, the players will eventually find a partner at the end of the string. If you want to come up girl/guy partners, mark one end of each long string with nail polish and give those to the girls.

5. **"I Went to the Mall."** Younger teens like this game. Ten guests sit in a circle and each is given a slip of paper with a word or phrase on it (hand them out in this order): fan, rocker, scissors, sewing machine, tight shoe, itchy new shirt, horse, sunglasses, perfume, cuckoo clock. The first person begins by saying, "I went to the mall and I bought a fan" and he starts fanning himself. All the others in the circle must then fan themselves. The second person says, "I went to the mall and bought a rocking chair." She starts rocking and the circle must continue fanning and also rock back and forth.

So it goes around the circle with each one adding their purchase and indicating the motion: fan with the left hand, rock the entire body, cut with the right hand, sew using the left foot, tap the floor with the right foot, squirm shoulders because of the itchy shirt, move up and down like a horse, blink because of the sun, sniff perfume, and say "cuckoo-cuckoo." It sounds silly but it looks even more silly. It's unlikely that everyone will be able to do all ten things simultaneously, but they'll have lots of fun trying.

6. **Robbery.** As guests arrive, privately ask each one to lend you something that belongs to her (glasses, earring, pen, dollar bill, lipstick, sock, and so forth.) For your own use, make a list of the items and the owners. In another room, place these items on a table (not in the order received) with a number by each one.

When everyone has arrived, announce that there have been robbers at work, but happily the loot has been located. Give each guest pencil and a paper numbered for the items. Let them all carefully observe the "stolen" items, trying to identify each with a guest. They are welcome to look at one another to see if they can determine if anything is missing. The winner is the one who gets the most stolen items correctly identified.

7. **Super Sleuths.** How reliable are the senses of touch, smell, and hearing? Give each guest a piece of paper and ask him to number it down the left side from one to thirty. (In advance, make your own answer list of the thirty items and prepare the items ahead.) Place the first ten items in sealed envelopes numbered one to ten. These will test the sense of touch. Make these ten the easiest, for example, key, small battery, paper clip, candy, lipstick, roll of mints, ring, safety pin, spool of thread, marble. The guests will pass the envelopes around, feeling them, and writing down what they think is inside.

Next, using the smallest containers you have (margarine dishes will do), label them from eleven to twenty, fill and cover them, making just a small slit in the lid. These will be passed around and sniffed to test the sense of smell: mouthwash, vanilla, vinegar, garlic juice, lemon juice, perfume, water, liquid soap, baby prunes, baby bananas. Guests do their best to identify these.

Finally to test the sense of hearing, have the guests sit directly in front of the host or hostess who has on a table a large box containing the final ten items, numbered twenty-one to thirty. The host will announce the number of the item (keeping it out of sight) and then "sound" it one time only: shuffling a deck of cards, crumpling a piece of paper, tapping two buttons together, cutting paper with scissors, knocking on a piece of wood, pulling off a piece of cellophane tape, zipping a zipper, clicking a ballpoint pen, pouring water from one cup to another, crunching a soda can. Again guests write down their guesses.

Finally, give the thirty answers and award a prize to the one with the best senses.

8. **The Coach's Nightmare.** Prepare for a simple basketball game in a gym, large backyard, or a driveway with a basketball hoop. Announce that there will be two teams—the girls versus the guys. The girls will be dressed normally. However, provide the guys with their basketball outfits: women's long dresses, high heels (old ones in case they break), and boxing gloves (or have each one tie one hand behind his back). It may be a nightmare—but a funny one.

"LET'S EAT"

Whatever you decide to serve, have plenty! In addition to menu ideas given above, here are some additional edibles teens will devour.

1. **Personal Pizza.** While kids of all ages love pizza, teens are the most creative in putting together fantastic combinations. Prepared pizza dough saves time and if you purchase the eight inch rounds, you can bake six to eight at one time, depending on your oven size.

Invite guests to the pizza bar where they assemble their personal creation. In addition to pizza sauce, have bowls of cheese, sliced pepperoni, browned ground beef, Canadian bacon, crushed drained pineapple, chopped olives, diced green chilis, mushrooms, sliced red onions, and other veggies.

2. **Chocolate Eclair Cake.** Here's a dessert both hearty and gooey—what more could a teen ask! *It must be made the day before and refrigerated,* or it can be made ahead, frozen, then thawed the day of the event. Preparation time is only about twenty minutes and it serves twelve.

Follow these steps:

1. Butter the bottom of a nine-by-thirteen-inch rectangular baking dish.
2. Cover the bottom with graham cracker squares, laid right next to each other. You'll use about fifteen squares.
3. Fix two small boxes of instant vanilla pudding according to the box instructions, *except* reduce milk to three cups total instead of four. Stir into the pudding an eight-to-twelve-ounce container of prepared whipped topping. (You can also use one box of instant vanilla pudding and one box of instant chocolate pudding— mixed separately—with four-to-six ounces of whipped topping in each.)
4. Put half of this mixture (or one flavor of pudding) on top of the graham cracker squares.
5. Cover with another layer of graham cracker squares.
6. Put remaining pudding mixture on top.
7. Cover with another layer of graham cracker squares. (This should use up most of one box.)
8. Frost with your own frosting (chocolate is good) or a round container of prepared frosting.
9. Cover tightly and refrigerate overnight.

3. **Fruit Slush.** Here's a great punch that *must* be made a day ahead. Depending on glass size, it will serve twenty to thirty. Mix in a *very* large bowl and then pour into large containers (such as gallon milk cartons with the tops cut off):

> 4 cups sugar
> 6 cups water
> 1 46 ounce can of pineapple juice
> 2 small cans of frozen orange juice concentrate
> 2 oranges, peeled and cut into chunks
> Juice of two lemons
> 5-6 bananas, mashed
> 2 bottles of maraschino cherries, cut in halves
> 1 box of fresh strawberries, halved, or 1 package of frozen sliced berries

Shake bottles, then freeze overnight. Remove from freezer two or three hours before serving (so juice is slushy). Fill each glass half full with the slush and fill the remainder with ginger ale. Serve with a straw. You can also put the slush in a punch bowl and add two bottles of ginger ale.

4. **"Eat Your Peas" Salad.** This takes about twenty minutes to prepare, but it's worth it since kids love it. It makes eight to ten servings and doubles easily.

Ingredients:

   ½ cup sour cream
   ½ cup mayonnaise
   2 tablespoons Dijon mustard
   2 tablespoons white wine vinegar
   ½ teaspoon dry tarragon
   ½ teaspoon ground nutmeg
   ½ teaspoon salt
   ¼ teaspoon pepper
   8 slices bacon, cooked until crisp
   1 small onion, finely chopped
   ⅓ pound mushrooms, thinly sliced
   2 10-ounce packages of frozen tiny peas, thawed
   1 head of butter lettuce

Method:

 While bacon is cooking, make the dressing: mix sour cream, mayonnaise, mustard, vinegar, tarragon, nutmeg, salt, and pepper. Set aside. Drain bacon, crumble, and refrigerate. Retain three tablespoons of the drippings and add the onion, cooking until limp. Add mushrooms and cook until soft. Remove from heat, transfer to serving bowl and stir in peas. Refrigerate this bowl and the dressing separately. Just before serving, mix in the dressing, arrange lettuce around the bowl edges, and sprinkle salad with bacon.

5. **Critter Crunch.** Here's a new twist to the trail mix or granola snacks—and you prepare it in just a few minutes. This recipe will serve a dozen teens:

Ingredients:

   ½ cup brown sugar
   1 stick margarine
   1 tablespoon cinnamon
   3 cups animal crackers
   3 cups bear-shaped honey-flavored graham crackers
   2 cups tiny pretzels
   3 cups corn or rice cereal squares
   3 cups toasted oat cereal
   2 cups bite-size whole wheat cereal biscuits with raisins

Method:

 Combine sugar and margarine in a bowl and microwave on high for one minute or until margarine melts and sugar dissolves. Stir in cinnamon. Combine the two kinds of crackers, the pretzels, and the three cereals. Spread in two nine-by-thirteen-inch baking dishes. Put half of the margarine mixture in each dish and toss gently until cereal mixture is coated. Bake at 350 degrees for twenty minutes, stirring once (check after fifteen minutes since ovens vary). Cool and serve, or store in a tightly covered container.

* * *

Teen party ideas can also be adapted from some of the adult parties described in chapter 3. Two that translate well to teen groups are the Time Capsule Party and the Pentathlon Party. And you'll want to consider making the spectacular Volcano Cake described in the same chapter. The Olympics Party in chapter 5 can also be modified—and made more competitive—for teens.

Don't be intimidated by the idea of entertaining teens. Their pseudo-sophistication about parties is often a cover-up for shyness. If your family sets a standard for more interesting get-togethers, you may soon find that other families with teens will host more creative parties at home—the best party environment there is.

7
Holiday Celebrations

While you'll usually entertain on a date of your own choosing, holidays provide a built-in excuse for a get-together on a specific date. While some holidays are just naturals for partying, this chapter will also introduce you to some unique holiday gatherings—giving you an entire year of memorable celebrations.

NEW YEAR'S DAY—THE RENAISSANCE PARTY

While parades and football games could make this holiday into a predictable routine, this New Year's Day Renaissance Party gives old traditions a new look. *Renaissance* means revival or being reborn, and this party celebrates the birth of a new year and the rebirth of hopes and dreams. You'll want to send written invitations well in advance so guests know the time schedule and have a few hints about what they can expect.

If this will be a large party, let guests bring some of the foods for the breakfast, the lunch, or the dessert buffet. This party adapts well for adults only or for families with children.

Early-bird breakfast. Start the party thirty minutes before the parade kick-off. Prepare a breakfast buffet of scrambled eggs and sausages kept warm in chafing dishes, assorted sweet rolls and doughnuts, a variety of juices, and coffee.

The parade. If there's a parade in your town, work it into the time schedule and attend as a group. If not, set up TVs so that guests can watch a big one such as Pasadena's Tournament of Roses. Give ballots to the guests so they can vote in these six categories: most beautiful float, most technically elaborate float, most humorous float, most unique float, most kid-oriented float, best marching band. At the end of the parade, let one person tally the ballots and determine the group's favorites. Award a prize (a calendar for the new year) to the person or persons who selected all six (or the most) favorites of the group.

Strike up the band. After watching the parade, it's time for some physical activity. In advance, gather simple musical instruments: kazoos, tambourines, triangles, maracas, sticks, even spoons. If guests can play an instrument, encourage them to bring it along. Borrow from the library a tape of march music to use on a portable player. Just like the bands in parades, line up and go marching around the house and right out the door. Be brave and serenade neighbors with your enthusiastic musical group!

Get ready for football. You'll need at least two television sets in separate rooms for now is the time to separate the serious (and silent) fans from those who want to both look and chat, or play card games or enjoy other amusements. Before the game begins, have everyone guess in various categories: the team to make the first score, halftime score, final score, the quarter when there is the first sack, fumble, or penalty. Award prizes of sports water bottles, visors, or mugs.

Game food. Use paper supplies so guests feel free to serve themselves often (and also to save yourself a major cleanup). Have plenty of chips and dips, hot dogs, baked beans or chili, fruit salad, beverages, as well as Cracker Jack and popcorn. Provide handy plastic-lined waste containers.

After the game. By now, the first day of the new year is well underway and it's time to think ahead. Have each guest write an anonymous New Year's resolution. This carries out the renaissance theme of starting fresh. Collect these for use later.

Dessert buffet. For some, this might be the last trip to the dessert table until the holiday pounds are shed! With the help of friends who like to make enticing desserts, offer a wide variety of these meal-enders and cut them into small pieces so that guests can sample several—or all.

Resolutions. During this calorie-consuming course, ask guests to sit in a circle. Place the resolutions written earlier in a bowl and let each person select one. Now go around the circle, letting each guest read the resolution selected. See if he can guess who wrote it. If he can't, go on to the next person. Gradually, by process of elimination, you should be able to identify the writer of each resolution.

The send-off. By this time, guests should be ready and able to face the new year, so send them on their way. And, if you've served alcohol, your last host duty is to be very sure there are designated drivers so that the year starts safely. Since this was a renaissance party, the guests should go home with the spirit of renewal and a zest for the new year.

VALENTINES' DAY—THE CANDY-LOVER'S PARTY

While we may think that this day is only for kids' school parties or for young lovers, it also can be celebrated as a fun-filled adult event held on February 14 or a nearby date.

Invitations: Buy inexpensive Valentines to use as the basis for announcing your Valentine dinner and chocolate-making party.

Food: Of course you'll want a red/pink/white dinner so consider baked ham, julienne beets, red-skinned potatoes, and a raspberry Jello and fruit mold with yogurt dressing (make pink with a few drops of food coloring). Top it off with cherry pie or cake à la mode.

Candy-making. Between dinner and dessert, assemble the guests in the kitchen to make these easy and yummy chocolate truffles. You'll need:

> 8 ounces of unsweetened chocolate (not chips)
> 4 ounces of semi-sweet chocolate (not chips)
> 1 14-ounce can of sweetened *condensed* milk
> 3 ounces of white chocolate for dipping
> 3 ounces of milk chocolate for dipping
> 1 tablespoon vegetable oil
> Toppings such as nuts, sprinkles, coconut, jimmies, nonpariels

Using a double boiler or the microwave, melt the unsweetened and semi-sweet chocolates and then stir in the condensed milk until smooth. For eight people (four teams of two), divide the mixture into four bowls and place these in the freezer for ten to fifteen minutes until the mixture starts to thicken.

Serve dessert during this break.

Now supply each team with a small cookie sheet lined with wax paper. Using teaspoons, the teams quickly make ball-shaped candies, about three-fourths inch in diameter, rolling half of these in nuts or other toppings and leaving half plain. Next, put the cookie sheets back in the freezer for about ten minutes.

In separate pans (or in the microwave), melt the white and milk chocolates and mix in the vegetable oil, making it smooth for coating. To finish the truffles without toppings, dip the top half of the cooled truffles in the white or milk chocolate. (A toothpick in the truffle can make this easy to do. You can also use another toothpick to drizzle one of these chocolates over the other.) Put the finished truffles back in the freezer for about five minutes.

Love Song Charades. While the candy is cooling, gather the guests together to play this game. Divide into twosomes. Let each couple think of a romantic song to act out. "People Will Say We're in Love," "The Look of Love," "All I Ask of You," "I'm in the Mood for Love," "My Funny Valentine" are a few ideas.

Then it's candy eating time!

ST. PATRICK'S DAY—THE SHAMROCK PARTY

It helps if you're Irish, but even if you have Swedish or Indian ancestors, plan an Irish-style party.

Invitations: Make your invitations out of green paper cut in the shape of a shamrock.

Ask guests to bring along the words to a favorite Irish song to sing during dinner. Some folks may have to go to the music store to find one.

Food: Of course the dinner should be the traditional corned beef, cabbage, potatoes, carrots, and bread.

Song time: It's not expensive to rent a karaoke machine—get one that will provide both the background music as well as the song sheets. After dinner, let each guest choose a favorite song—some choices will be Irish songs, others will be popular tunes. Start the singing yourself or choose someone who you know has a good voice to sing first. As the songs continue, musical ability will mean less than good fun. Soon everyone will want to get into the act and it's amazing how good even the tone-deaf sound!

APRIL FOOL'S DAY—THE PRANKS PARTY

Both kids and adults enjoy pranks, so build your party around clever tricks. Encourage each guest to bring a prank to do in the course of the evening, but prepare some yourself:
* Reset the clocks around the house for an hour later.
* Don't use the dining table; put place mats and settings under the table and have guests eat on the floor.
* At a party shop, get plastic ice cubes with bugs in them for use in the beverages.
* Place rubber lizards in surprising places.
* Sprinkle wide rubber bands on top of a tossed salad (so people will notice them and not eat them).
* Hide a noisy alarm clock in the centerpiece and set it to go off during the supper.
* Put a nut in the dessert and give a prize to the person who finds it.
* Put a paper cup of water on top of the bathroom door as a surprise when someone shuts the door. (Have paper towels handy in the bathroom for a quick mop up so no one will slip.)
* Play recordings of the crazy music of Spike Jones (and if you don't know this old-time group, it's time you did). Borrow one of his recordings from the library.

While you are doing these pranks, your guests will be doing theirs, too. Anything goes as long as it isn't mean or dangerous. To add to the evening, you could show a video of David Copperfield doing his extravagant magic tricks.

EASTER: A PARTY FOR GOOD EGGS

Of course there's egg coloring and hunting, but you can have a creative Easter party that includes those ideas with innovative variations and also introduces a few different traditions. It works well as a breakfast, brunch, or supper event.

Invitations: Hand-deliver invitations made from real eggs. Pierce each end of an egg and gently blow out the contents (useful for scrambled eggs). Color the eggs. Then using small sharp scissors, such as cuticle scissors, cut out a large oval portion of one side of the shell to make a window. In tiny print, write your invitation on paper and glue it inside the egg window. Decorate the eggs further if you wish. Put each egg in a small box packed with tissue and hand deliver to invitees.

The Easter Tree. Before the party, find a large multibranched tree limb or a small dead tree. Remove any leaves and prune to a pleasing shape. Using quick-set cement or plaster, plant the tree securely in a pot and then spray paint it white or another color of your choice.

Have plenty of blown-out eggs and decorations (glitter, tiny beads, stickers, colored paper, marking pens, ribbon, glue) ready for the guests to use. Each person creates an egg and then, using the ribbon and glue, hangs it on the tree. It makes a great centerpiece or focal point.

The Pancake Race: This began in England where it was a Lenten tradition for women carrying skillets to race while tossing pancakes in the air. (This race is also mentioned as part of a pancake party for teens in chapter 6.) Make a race course about fifty feet long with a chair or other large object at the end. Prepare pancakes about five inches in diameter, and use two same-size skillets. Divide the group into two teams for the relay race. The object is to run the race course, around the chair, and back to the start line while flipping the pancake in the skillet at least one time. (A dropped pancake means that the racer must start over.) When a racer returns to the starting line, the next one on the team starts doing the same thing. Prizes for the winners could be small bottles of syrup. The losers get to do the dishes after the meal.

The Meal: Since this is a party for good eggs, make a soufflé or quiche as your main dish to be served with various fruits, turkey sausage, and bacon. An angel or sunshine cake will carry out your egg theme. Many of these recipes can be made with cholesterol-free eggs.

If you prefer a pancake theme, you can invite guests into your kitchen to help make the pancakes to be served with many toppings.

MAY DAY—THE FLOWER POWER PARTY

While this party is usually a women's luncheon event, there's no reason why men can't enjoy it, too. There are just two elements: food and flowers.

Because you'll need lots of flowers, you may want to find a local flower market, or a friendly farmer with a field of wildflowers. One party-giver goes to a local florist and gets excess flowers practically free. Or perhaps your own garden will yield enough flowers and greenery.

Invitations: Press colorful small flowers until they are dried (this will take about a week for single flowers placed between paper towels and under the weight of a heavy book). Then glue them to note cards to make the invitations. Ask each invitee to bring a vase and small garden clippers.

Flower Arranging: Have pails of water filled with flowers, branches, and other greenery—sufficient for the size of the group. Have plenty of "Oasis" type arranging material on hand so that flowers will stay where they are put. Provide work spaces such as kitchen counters and card tables covered with newspapers, or, in good weather, use outside picnic or patio tables. Place a large rubbish container in a convenient place.

Place a small card with each guest's name in various locations suitable for showing off an arrangement: tables, mantle, chest of drawers, shelves, and so forth. When each guest has found the location for her arrangement, the actual arranging begins. Finished arrangements are put in their designated places so that all can view them. Put a ribbon award by *each* arrangement: most beautiful, creative, colorful, clever, amusing, exquisite, original, and so forth.

The Food: Did you know that violets, nasturtiums and pansies are among the many edible flowers? (Rinse them first!) Make the luncheon a floral event with open-faced sandwiches of cream cheese and jam topped with edible flowers edged with tiny bits of parsley, mint, or watercress. Serve these elegant sandwiches with a fruit salad decorated with flowers. For dessert, have a cake decorated with frosting flowers.

Each guest takes home the arrangement she made plus any extra flowers.

MOTHER'S DAY—A FAMILY PARTY

The location for this party is the bedroom! It takes place early on Mother's Day and the preparation involves everyone in the family except Mom (who should pretend to be asleep). When the family has breakfast ready, they awaken Mom by strewing her bed with rose petals!

Breakfast Party Food: Who says that you can't have cake for breakfast? But before the cake, consider simplified Eggs Benedict (a toasted English muffin topped with low-fat sour cream, Canadian bacon, poached egg, and cheese—put briefly under the broiler) served with juice and coffee. Then the cake, made or purchased in advance and kept hidden from Mom.

The Gifts: While a trip to Hawaii might be Mom's dream gift, here are some less expensive alternatives: a plant for home or office, a bread machine, colorful socks or scarves, tickets for an event, a gift certificate for a spa visit, a framed family photo, a pen and pencil set, a big coffee-table candle, cologne (you can't have too much and it keeps).

The Events: Since this is a Sunday, you may want to go to church together, then to lunch, and a movie. Also consider a walk in the park, a game of Monopoly, and supper in the living room (soup and biscuits by the fire are nice). And some moms would enjoy a facial, back, or foot massage.

You can share the after-breakfast events with families of good friends who are also celebrating Motherhood.

MEMORIAL DAY—THE HISTORICAL PARTY

A holiday honoring the dead doesn't sound like a barrel of laughs, and of course it isn't, but it can still be the foundation for a party among good friends. If the weather permits, let this be a barbecue event on the patio or porch, or if it's too cold, gather around the fire in the living room.

The following Memorial Day facts are ones you can use as a quiz game by dividing the group into two teams and awarding points for correct answers.

1. Following what war did the Memorial Day tradition begin? (Civil War)
2. Who first started this commemoration? (Southern women)
3. Why was it called Decoration Day? (The women placed ribbons and flowers on military graves.)
4. What flower became associated with this holiday? (Red poppy)
5. What's the connection of the poppy? (It symbolizes the poppy fields in France where many American soldiers gave their lives.)

6. Who sold artificial poppies for many years to aid disabled comrades? (Veterans groups)
7. What year did this day become a federal holiday—1951, 1961, 1971? (1971)
8. How is the date selected? (It is always the last Monday in May)
9. What is a tradition in port cities? (Toy ships filled with flowers are set afloat.)
10. Where is a local celebration held? (Check your local paper for this answer.)
11. What is the traditional music played at these services? (Taps)
12. Where does the President lay a wreath? (Arlington National Cemetery at the Tomb of the Unknowns)
13. What is a good idea for promoting peace in the world?
14. What is a good idea for promoting peace in our community?
15. What is a good idea for promoting peace in our family?

Good food, good friends, and good ideas can make this party meaningful.

FLAG DAY—A FLAGS-OF-ALL-NATIONS PARTY

Although this day honors the American flag, it's fun to know more about flags of other countries. Be sure to decorate with U.S. flags and patriotic colored streamers inside and outside your house.

Invitations: Use red and blue ribbons and stickers to decorate your white paper invitations. When the guests respond, ask each one what country their ancestors came from.

Place Cards: With an encyclopedia as a picture reference, and using colored construction paper and markers or crayons, make flags of these countries about three inches by five inches in size. Put these on the table as place cards. You may have to help guests find their places to sit if they don't recognize their flags!

Activities: After dinner, let each guest tell about ancestral traditions that are still honored in their family.

Concerning the American flag, see who can tell when the flag is *not* to be flown, two ways to salute the flag, the meaning of an upside-down flag, where a flag goes on a speaker's platform, when it is flown at half-staff, how to fold a flag military style, and what happens to old flags. (Your flag store, encyclopedia, or Scout Handbook will give you this information.)

As a take-home gift, provide small U.S. flags for guests to place on their car antennas—they look patriotic and also can help locate a car in a crowded parking lot!

FATHER'S DAY—THE KING-FOR-A-DAY PARTY

Celebrate this day with as many fathers and grandfathers (your own relatives or good friends) as you can find. The theme is "King-for-a-Day" and the kids can make crowns for the dads and granddads out of cardboard and foil. The day may start with gifts and breakfast in bed, but the real party comes later in the day.

Location: Don't tell Dad, but arrange for the party to be at a ballgame, park, or outdoor theater. In secret, arrange for other families with dads to be there. Keep the food hidden, the tickets out-of-sight. Then, at the appropriate time, suggest that the family go for a ride and take Dad to the site of his party.

Activities: In advance, buy matching T-shirts for all the men to wear at the party. Activities at a park could be: relay races, tug-of-war, and a treasure hunt in which all the participants are clued-in to let the dads win.

If the party is at a ballgame, have guessing contests for the player to make the first hit, for the inning with the most runs, for the player who steals, for the attendance, and for the final score. Women and kids should have funds to treat the dads to refreshments.

If the party is at an event with an intermission, use that time for gift-giving.

Gifts: Anything but ties! If you're considering a major gift for a dad who works in an office, assemble an "executive kit" in a new briefcase. Fill it with a calendar, new pens, paper clips, rubber stamps, Post-it notes, envelopes, letterhead, a granola bar, and (of course) a new picture of the family for his desk.

Other gifts can be a new cap, mug, sports equipment, barbecue utensils, magazine subscription, electric tool, jazzy socks, homemade coupons for a home-style car wash, or tickets to an event.

INDEPENDENCE DAY—AN OLD-FASHIONED FOURTH

Send your invitations early so that guests have time to plan their participation. In each family or couple attending, one person can help with the food, the other can be a speech maker or a game organizer. This is an old-fashioned everyone-pitches-in kind of party.

Location: Have it in a big yard (or park) with plenty of tables, chairs, and umbrellas. A small pool or slip-and-slide for the kids is fun. Make a real "soap box" (the speaker's platform) bedecked in red, white, and blue. Be sure to decorate with flags and bunting.

Food: The menu can consist of ribs, hamburgers, or hot dogs served with potato salad, macaroni salad, sweet corn, and watermelon. Pink lemonade is a must.

Activities: Events can include a two-legged race, a barrel race, a pie-eating contest, a race on stilts, tug-of-war, and a watermelon eating (or seed spitting) contest.

For background music, play recordings of Sousa marches and patriotic songs.

The main event is the speeches. Those assigned to speak can choose any topic—political, economic, humorous, patriotic. (Be sure to have at least one of each by asking the topic when guests RSVP.) No speech should last more than three minutes. Encourage lots of applause and hollering—even for bad speeches!

At the end of the party, gather to sing "America, the Beautiful" or "God Bless America."

If your community permits it, sparklers or other simple fireworks, safely ignited only by the adults, can end the day.

LABOR DAY—THE SUNRISE CELEBRATION

To many, this holiday signals the end of summer fun and back-to-school, so it can be a bittersweet one unless you plan a party to cheer family and friends.

Choose the Location: Essential to this party is a hill, mountaintop, or lake, with a good view toward the east. Easy parking and picnic facilities are necessary.

Invitees: Choose guests who have a sense of adventure—people willing to get up early in the morning to experience something memorable. Tell them to bring binoculars, sunglasses, lawn chairs or blankets, jackets, paper, and drawing materials.

Activities: Watching the first hints of dawn and then seeing the sun explode on the horizon is a great thrill. Check the newspaper for the time of sunrise and plan to *be at your destination an hour in advance.*

Set up your camp so that everyone can see clearly and comment on the changing eastern sky. Notice every little difference: the first glow, the outline of a distant hill, a tree coming into view. Encourage a big "hooray" when the sun first breaks above the horizon. Be aware of things unseen before: animals, houses, people.

Now, let everyone make a drawing of his impression of the sunrise—you'll be surprised at how unique each picture is.

Breakfast: When the fascination of dawn wears off, serve breakfast (made the night before)—all things that tie in with the round sun and the yellow and orange colors of dawn: full slices of oranges, bagels with cream cheese, cornbread, round granola cookies, bananas, and orange-lemonade. A thermos of hot coffee may also be welcome. Make the food easy to serve and eat, and easy to clean up since Labor Day should mean NO labor for you.

After breakfast, make up rhymes by providing the first line and letting others suggest a rhyming line. Here are a few to get you started: I saw the sun (and it was fun). It was dark (in the park). We sat up high (to see the sky). It is no joke (the sun's an egg yolk). Dawn was great (but was a wait). Sunrise is a treat (but I'd rather eat).

On the way home, talk about the origin of Labor Day—the labor movement and the importance of honest work and fair rewards.

GRANDPARENTS' DAY—SECOND SUNDAY IN SEPTEMBER

Grandparents today are not just sitting and rocking on the porch—they are active people, probably into computers and some might even be "surfing the net" or out in the waves enjoying real surfing. So, the theme of a party honoring them can be quite contemporary.

To make it special, it needs the input of the grandkids, both near and far. Select in advance a time when out-of-town grandchildren will telephone to wish the grandparents a happy day. Be sure that on this day grandma doesn't have to cook anything!

Events: Encourage grandchildren to present a play depicting the life of the grandparents from childhood to the present time. Tell them a few facts and let them take it from there—this makes it funny as two youngsters play the roles of their grandparents. Don't let them rehearse too much—the more improvised the better.

Play "Did you know?" with grandparents asking questions for the group to answer, for example: "What year were we married?" "What was Grandma's first job?" "How many houses have we lived in?" "What's Grandpa's favorite food?"

Food. Each grandchild can contribute to the meal with guidance from parents, making a family favorite: a salad, bread, veggies and dip, or a decorated cake. The adults can provide the main dish and beverages.

Gifts: Gifts for the honorees can be theater or sports tickets, a selection of greeting cards with stamps, framed photos, telephone call certificates, a magazine subscription, or a book of handmade certificates good for tasks such as snow shoveling, weeding, closet cleaning, car washing, and so forth.

Be sure to take a photo of the group for the family album.

HALLOWEEN—AN AUTUMN CELEBRATION

Witches and devils are giving way to less scary costumes and parties that don't require candy-begging in order to be fun. Parents are learning that for young children, there's no merit in scaring them with horror pictures and stuffing them with sweets.

Let Halloween become a celebration of the autumn season. These ideas will make your party fun and not frightening for young children, as well as enjoyable for older kids and adults.

Decorations: Use bales of hay for seating and autumn leaves for table decor. Hollow-out pumpkins and put candles in them for light. To welcome guests at the front door, make a scarecrow out of a simple wood frame, old clothes stuffed for fullness, and a pumpkin head.

Costumes: Since scary, gory costumes are no longer popular, consider a new party theme such as "Dress like a movie, TV, or cartoon star." Some good ideas are Charlie Chaplin, Batman, Daisy Mae, and for a group: 101 Dalmatians or the California raisins. Other costume themes could be outerspace, favorite animals, babies, and music groups. Be sure to have prizes for the best costumes.

Activities:

1. **Play "Name That Tune":** Select about twenty-five songs in advance and gather recordings or sheet music. The group sits in a circle with a bell in the middle. Using recordings or a live piano player picking out the tune, play about five seconds of a song. The first to leap up and ring the bell, and give the right answer gets a point.
2. **Tunnel Races.** This tunnel is a favorite of youngsters, but great fun for adults,

too. Using five yards of jersey tube material as a tunnel, let everyone climb through just to get the feel. (You will need two people to hold the ends.) Then, divide the group into teams for relay races, one team starting from each end. This is especially hilarious when two people struggle to pass each other at midpoint.

3. **Pumpkin Carving Contest.** Divide into teams of two for artistic planning and carving. For each team, provide a medium-sized pumpkin, marking pen, and knife, plus a ring of cardboard for the jack-o-lantern's collar. Vote for the most creative and give a prize of pumpkin seed snacks.

4. **Pumpkin Race.** This relay race requires two small round pumpkins, two teams, and a start and finish line about twenty feet apart. The object for each racer is to get on hands and knees and push the pumpkin to the finish line using only her head (no hands). At the finish line, she picks up the pumpkin and takes it back to the start line for the next racer. The game can also be played by using a broom to push the pumpkin. You'll find that the irregular shape of pumpkins make them difficult and funny to manage.

5. **Country Dancing.** An excellent two-generation activity. At the library or from friends, borrow recordings for square dancing, country line dancing, Virginia Reel, and so forth. Books are available if you need to bone-up on the steps. Don't hesitate to actually teach a dance.

Food: An autumn party calls for a hearty menu such as ribs, beans with hot dogs, or chili served over baked potatoes or spaghetti, with toppings of cheese, sour cream, and green onions. Hot apple cider with cinnamon sticks is a tasty hot drink and for a seasonal dessert give a choice of pumpkin or apple pie.

Prizes: Depending on age, prizes can be bags of candy corn or other trick-or-treat goodies, candied apples, small pumpkins, and autumn flowers such as mums. Consider also "awarding" the bales of hay at the end of the party.

THANKSGIVING—THE CELEBRATION OF GRATITUDE

While your Thanksgiving party will probably be built around a huge meal, consider these ideas to de-emphasize gorging and give your celebration a refreshing look. Be sure to extend your invitations early, and, if it's a large group, ask guests to bring part of the feast.

Recreate an old-time menu. Who says it has to be turkey and cranberries? Consider returning to the roots of this holiday by planning an early American menu. You may want to mix traditional foods with these more unusual dishes. Popular main dishes back then included lobster, duck, goose, clams, oysters, eel, and venison. Instead of stuffing there were popcorn, pancakes, and cornbread. Steamed or baked vegetables included whole beans, squash, watercress, onions, and leeks. The final course was probably not pumpkin pie, but more likely baked pumpkin and dried sweetened fruits.

Design cornucopia place cards. Use ice-cream cones (the pointed sugar cones) as mini horns of plenty. Tie a gold bow around the opening of the cone and with a decorator tube of icing (available at the market), write the name of the invitee on the cone. Place each cone on a small rectangular card on the table. Fill the cone with small fruits and fruit-shaped candies (grapes, cherries, candy corn, raspberry and marzipan candies) so that they appear to tumble out of the cornucopia.

Make a "Grateful Chain." While family and friends are gathering, provide colorful strips of construction paper, pens, and a stapler. Let guests write—no need to sign—the simple or profound things they are grateful for, and then staple them into a chain. (Many families start the Grateful Chain in early November and add to it daily, making a very long chain that winds up the staircase or across the dining room.) During dessert, read the chain aloud—some contributions will be silly (but still sincere), others will be quite touching.

The Corn Eating Race. Using frozen corn on the cob, have a cooked ear of corn for each participant. The object is to see who can eat the fastest. You'll need a judge to start the race and to verify that every kernel has been eaten from the cob, and swallowed.

Plan a Day-Long Celebration. My family has long celebrated Thanksgiving as a day-long event and you may wish to adopt some of our traditions. Our invitation includes the full schedule and assignments for guests to direct certain activities, bring specific foods, do kitchen cleanup or table setting, thus no one person is overworked.

1. **Surfer's Breakfast.** As we live near the ocean, the day starts early with surfing. However, even nonsurfers gather for our traditional breakfast of muffins hot from the oven, cheesy scrambled eggs, and three kinds of melon slices.

2. **Church.** This *is* the day for gratitude and we gather at church for that purpose. If you aren't near a church with a Thanksgiving service, you can hold your own.

3. **Photo Opportunity.** It isn't often that the entire family—complete with the newest babies—are all together in one place. So be sure to take lots of snapshots, plus a posed picture of the entire group.

4. **Game Time.** As our weather is usually warm, we have a volleyball game while the finishing touches are being given to the dinner. (In cold climates, use this time to make the Grateful Chain described above.)

5. **The Feast.** The dining room table and added card tables let all twenty-five of us be together as one happily crowded group. The turkey, stuffing, and gravy are prepared at our house and all the other foods are brought by relatives and friends. With the buffet ready, one person (who has been asked in advance) gives the grace— and then we eat! Little gifts are given to the new members of the family and to the first person to RSVP (part of my plan to encourage good manners among the next generation). Then, before dessert, we have a story and joke-a-thon with prizes. (Many family members search all year for what they hope will be the winning contribution!)

6. **Do Your Own Thing Time.** At this point there are naps for young and old, walks in the fresh air, and time for more volleyball or other games.

7. **Photo Contest.** Everyone brings his best photo in three categories: adult, child, or scenic. These are numbered and put on large poster boards where all can see them. Later everyone votes for their favorites in each category, and photo album prizes are awarded the winners.

8. **New Game.** Since many of the attenders have children, we always test a new game. Many of the games in this book were first tried on Thanksgiving Day; the string maze (page 88), the conveyor belt (page 74), and the ballooney sandwich (page 67) are a few.

9. **Piñata.** The bashing of a piñata is a custom the Pilgrims never thought of. The papier-machâ turkey is filled with goodies and we draw numbers, are blindfolded, and try to break it open with a baseball bat. For the kids, it's the highlight of the day!

10. **Snapping Game.** While supper is being prepared, the group plays this game, described on page 88. Since we've been playing it for decades, we have a silly roving trophy for the winner.

11. **Supper Buffet.** This includes salads and breads (brought by others) to go with the leftovers from the main meal. And, it's topped off with a variety of the first-of-the-season Christmas cookies.

12. **Music Time.** By now, semi-immobile due to food and games, everyone's winding

down and group singing is the entertainment answer—songs of several generations.

13. **Uncle Cliff's Video.** My husband saves (on videotape) snippets of the funniest things we've seen on television during the past year, and he presents his masterpiece. Other presentations brought by guests have included videos of new babies, skiing trips, hurricane survival, and the star of the school play—that all are "required" to see.

14. **Circle of Light.** As families pack up for the night, we gather with small candles to form a circle of light. Then, one-by-one, we extinguish the candles and the families go their separate ways.

CHRISTMAS—PARTIES THAT SHARE LOVE

Christmas offers numerous opportunities for innovative entertaining and it is sad that so many gatherings are merely dull cocktail parties or routine family feasts. I've written an entire book on the subject of a more meaningful Christmas and in it you'll find many usable ideas. The book is titled *101 Ideas for the Best-Ever Christmas* (Nashville: Dimensions for Living, 1992) and it includes party themes, crafts and gifts as well as new Christmas stories.

Here are just a few party ideas to enliven your holiday events.

1. **The Christmas Family.** Through a religious or social service group, obtain the names, ages, and description of a needy family. In your party invitation, assign guests to be "Christmas angels" to individual members of the family or to bring foods and decorations for the entire family. For example, one guest couple may be assigned seven-year-old Karen who wants a doll or a bike helmet. Another guest can be assigned canned goods or a small Christmas tree.

The folks go shopping on their own and at the party all the purchases are shared. Then paper is supplied to giftwrap the items and boxes are ready to be packed with foods and decorations. In some cases, you will bring your items to the agency, in others you will be permitted to deliver them directly to the family.

Following the packing of the gifts and supplies, serve a buffet supper based on the traditions of another country. If you need ideas, you'll find holiday celebrations from fourteen countries described in my Christmas book.

2. **The Caroling Party.** This kind of party is ideal for mixing old friends with new acquaintances. Obtain or make song sheets of about twenty-five Christmas songs—some traditional carols, some new songs. Give variety to the singing by providing bells to sing with "Jingle Bells," choosing three soloists for "We Three Kings," or acting out "The Twelve Days of Christmas." A proficient accompanist (an essential element of this party) should preview the carols.

Here's a game that will tie in with your caroling party. Just make a copy of this page for each guest.

Provide a special ornament or Christmas audiotape as a prize for the winner of this game.

ANSWERS: 1. Jingle Bells 2. Walking in a Winter Wonderland 3. Santa Claus Is Coming to Town 4. Joy to the World 5. Rudolph, the Red-nosed Reindeer 6. O Come, All Ye Faithful 7. I'm Dreaming of a White Christmas 8. O Christmas Tree 9. What Child Is This? 10. We Three Kings 11. Deck the Halls 12. I Saw Three Ships 13. O Holy Night 14. Noel 15. Away in a Manger 16. The Twelve Days of Christmas 17. I Saw Mama Kissing Santa Claus 18. All I Want for Christmas Is My Two Front Teeth 19. Chestnuts Roasting on an Open Fire 20. It Came Upon a Midnight Clear 21. Let It Snow, Let It Snow.

3. **The Cookie Party.** Invite about twenty friends (or ten couples) to come to a party early in December. Ask guests to make a quantity of their favorite cookie (about sixty of one kind) plus copies of the recipe. Suggest they bring spare cookie tins so they can take cookies safely home. Each guest will give and receive cookies—a great way to get an immediate supply of a variety of cookies and of course, to enjoy some new ones.

As guests gather, have a jelly bean contest. Using a clear glass jar with lid, count out the quantity of red and green jelly beans that it takes to fill the jar. Everyone guesses and the nearest answer wins a prize. The jelly bean jar is given later to a school, church, or charity for holiday snacking.

The host will have made in advance simple sugar cookies—some large, some small. Have various frostings, decorator tubes, sprinkles, and candies available for decorating the large ones and give a prize for the best-decorated cookie. Serve them with cider or hot chocolate.

Use the small cookies to decorate a gingerbread house to give to a school, care facility, or hospital. You can make the house from a small cardboard box with cut-out doors and windows, plus a square cardboard chimney. Use gingerbread cake mix baked until very firm in large shallow pans to obtain the thin flat slabs that you will affix to the sides with frosting. Then, with icing tubes, add trim around doors and windows, and flowers along the bottom edges. The small cookies make a perfect roof.

Attendants leave this party feeling that they've contributed to the joy—and the sweet tooth—of others, but have also amassed for themselves a wonderful variety of cookies for the holidays.

4. **The Gifts for a King.** This party is about giving, but not spending! When everyone is so busy and often budget-weary, this party is the answer.

Invite many guests, but be sure you know one another since you will bring a special gift for one of the other guests. The host/hostess assigns each guest's name to another guest who will then "go shopping" in his house, garage, attic, basement, or office to find something that will have meaning to that person. Items are *not* to be white elephants or junk, but perhaps something the other person has admired or something of value that no longer fits your home and style. This gift exchange should be the last event at the party.

In advance of your party, contact a social services organization and get the name of an institution or family that would welcome a three-foot-tall trimmed Christmas tree. Buy the tree and a variety of sizes of styrofoam balls, sequins, beads, straight pins, ribbons, and sparkle glue for making ornaments. As examples, make one or two ornaments in advance and hang them on the tree set up in the party room. When guests gather, they make and trim the tree with their handmade ornaments. Since the tree is small and the ornaments are not breakable, it will travel easily to its destination.

While making the decorations, play the Twisted Titles game. One person will read the twisted title (a carol translated into other words) and the first person to correctly state it wins a point. (You don't need to make any copies, just read from this book.)

1. The lad is a miniature percussionist (Little Drummer Boy)
2. Embellish the entryways (Deck the Halls)
3. Overhead on shingles (Up on the Rooftop)
4. Leave and broadcast from a pinnacle (Go Tell It on the Mountain)
5. Present me naught but dual incisors for this festive holiday (All I Want for Christmas Is My Two Front Teeth)
6. Far back in the hay bin (Away in a Manger)
7. 288 Yuletide Hours (Twelve Days of Christmas)
8. Do we both perceive the same longitudinal pressure on our auditory organs? (Do You Hear What I Hear?)
9. As guardians of wooly animals protected their charges during earth's darkness (While Shepherds Watched Their Flocks by Night)
10. Listen, winged heavenly messengers are proclaiming tunefully (Hark, the Herald Angels Sing)
11. The Supreme Being gives respite to joyful distinguished males (God Rest You Merry Gentlemen)
12. Obese personification, fabricated of a compressed amount of minute crystals (Frosty the Snowman)
13. The Christmas preceding all others (The First Noel)
14. Natal celebration devoid of vivid color (White Christmas)
15. Geographic state of fantasy during the season of Mother Nature's dormancy (Winter Wonderland)
16. Jovial Yuletide desired for the second person singular or plural by us (We Wish You a Merry Christmas)
17. Accept for your own being a cheerful minute holiday celebration (Have Yourself a Merry Little Christmas)
18. Expected arrival at this location by mythical masculine gift-giver (Here Comes Santa Claus)
19. A twitter-pating sound made by metallic vessels which vibrate when shaken (Jingle Bells)

5. **Stuff Santa Party.** This works well for a group of adults *and* children.

First, you'll need Santa's reindeer. Have a supply of brown poster board. Cut some in advance to make headbands: two-inch wide lengths to go around both adult and child-size heads. Each guest staples the headband to her size, then cuts her own antlers out of cardboard and decorates them with glitter and glue, stapling them to her headband. Now properly dressed, the gifts for good girls and boys come next.

In advance, take the favors to be given at the end of the party and put them in boxes. Tape the boxes shut. Divide into teams (one adult, one youngster works well) and give each twosome two boxes to wrap, wrapping paper, tape, and ribbon or yarn. They are to work together to properly wrap the two gifts, however, they are to use only left hands (left-handers will use right hands). It's not easy! The wrappers of the package that is judged best wrapped get to be first to choose a package to take home.

For stuffing Santas, you'll need two extra-large size union suits dyed red, two Santa hats, and lots of balloons. Guests are divided into two teams with the object of creating the stoutest Santa. One team member wears the suit and the others get busy blowing up balloons and gently stuffing them inside Santa's arms, legs, back, and especially front. Of course, some balloons will break. Set a timer for ten minutes and do take pictures of the two chunky Santas. The winning team is the next to choose party favor boxes, the losers are last.

NEW YEAR'S EVE—FAREWELL FUN

No more is year-end an occasion for drunken revelry (at least it shouldn't be!). Parties that celebrate the old and new year can be creative, enjoyable, and exuberant. These ideas will enliven parties for both adults and youngsters. You will get other ideas from the New Year's Day party described at the beginning of this chapter.

1. **Mystery Sacks Party.** This event does a great job of mixing old and new friends. Guests are instructed to bring an item (hidden in a sack) that represents something they would like to do in their free time during the new year. These are collected and then redistributed. The receiver looks at the item and then keeps the contents secret from everyone else.

Then the games begin. Each guest is given a rotation schedule of game stations and will spend about thirty minutes at each station. The stations are in various rooms: Ping-Pong in the family room or garage, an outdoor basketball shoot, Trivial Pursuit, Rummy Royale, Yahtzee, and so forth. As guests move from game to game, they carry their sacks, and can engage in conversations with the other guests, asking questions about hobbies, lifestyle, and so forth, but they may not directly ask "Did you bring the ———?"

Before midnight, the group gathers in one place. Each person shows the item in the sack they've been carrying about and tells who they think it belongs to. Correct guesses are given horns for blowing at midnight, losers get confetti to throw.

2. **Midnight Cake.** Make a large round layer cake with filling and frosting. Then, using decorator icing tubes, put a clock face on the top with the hands of the clock pointing to five minutes before midnight. It makes an attractive (and delicious) table centerpiece. Surround the cake with battery-operated alarm clocks, all set to go off at midnight.

3. **Resolutions.** If you spend New Year's Eve with the same group each year, give invitees paper, pencil, and envelope for writing a New Year's resolution. Have writers seal their envelopes and then put all the individual envelopes in one large envelope that is also sealed with sturdy tape. Entrust the most responsible person to take the envelope home and keep it for the next New Year's Eve party when it will be opened. It will be interesting to see how many carried out their resolutions.

4. **Practical Pachyderms.** A white-elephant exchange is good party fun, but give it a new twist. As usual, each guest will bring one white elephant item, gift wrapped. However, specify that it should be something that can be used in the new year (a large calendar, a scale for dieters, a dreadful tie to be worn on April Fool's Day, a decorator item, or a coupon for an upcoming event).

All the wrapped gifts are put in the center of the circle of guests. Numbers are drawn for the order of selecting gifts. The person drawing #1 chooses first, opens the gift, and must tell how he will use it in the new year. Then, the person with #2 does the same thing—however, after opening it, he can trade his chosen gift with the one already opened. This continues until all gifts have been selected and many traded. Then, the person with #1 gets the final trade for his favorite gift.

5. **Midnight Walk.** At fifteen minutes to midnight, encourage guests to put on their coats for a walk outside. Take a radio along, tuned to a station that will give the countdown to the next year. Give a loud cheer, look up at the stars, and say a silent thank you for the previous year's blessings. Then greet the new year with kisses all around.

* * *

You will find more ideas for parties adaptable to the holidays in chapters 3, 4, 5, and 6.

Special Occasion?
No Occasion? Party!

S ometimes a special occasion calls for a celebration: your good friends are marrying, having a baby, celebrating an anniversary or retirement, or embarking on a long-awaited trip. Other times, you just have the desire to *create* an occasion that calls for a party. Don't be shy—just do it!

Here are ideas for those times when you want to enjoy the company of new or old friends.

WELCOME TO THE NEIGHBORHOOD

In our mobile society, it seems there is always someone moving in or moving out of the neighborhood. Use these occasions as reasons for get-togethers.

1. **Barbecue Get-Together.** Welcoming a family to the neighborhood is a caring and friendly event. Because everyone is curious to meet the new neighbors, why not have a weekend barbecue party? On poster board, make a large diagram of your area. As guests arrive, let them indicate where they live and write in their address, names of family members, names of pets, as well as their own jobs and hobbies. You may want to add some of the ideas in the following party descriptions.

2. **For Women Only.** A more formal event is a women's luncheon that I once gave to welcome a new resident. In the invitation, I enclosed a three-by-five card and requested that attenders describe on the card two things: an interesting local site and a good restaurant. As each guest arrived, a picture of her with the guest of honor was taken. One person was assigned to assemble a welcome book with a page for

each neighbor's photo and her information card. The book provided a way of identifying new friends and also a means of getting to know the new city. After the luncheon, each guest shared how her family happened to choose this area as their new home.

3. **A Special Welcome.** This party was given for a new widower with three children who moved into a condominium. The neighbors asked if they could come to say hello on a Sunday afternoon. Each dropped in with a casserole dish that could be eaten or frozen, and a recipe card for the dish. By the end of the afternoon, his family had many new friends and some wonderful meals to enjoy plus the recipes so they could reproduce them.

One couple who had been warmly welcomed into their new neighborhood now have a yearly supper party on the anniversary of their moving-in day.

GRADUATION CELEBRATIONS

Although there are often school-related parties solely for the grads, a family may want to honor a graduate with an open house, luncheon, or dinner event.

For a College Grad. A friend of mine called such a party "Welcome to the Real World" and invited the grad's relatives, neighbors, and other good friends. A U-shaped table was set up in the family room to accommodate the twenty-four guests and let them all be at the same table as the grad. The buffet featured both steak and beans as symbolic of the feast-or-famine days ahead.

The parents had prepared a video production called "This Is Your Crazy Life." It was created from old slides and photos that they had turned into a video of the grad's growing up years. The final activity was the presentation of gifts from the guests— gifts that would be useful in the real world he was now entering. These included a basic cookbook, an alarm clock, a bus pass, a tie, an appointment book, a spelling-checker, a downtown area map, quick energy bars, a broom, and a cassette tape on how to succeed in business.

For a Grade-School Graduate. Parents of one grad surprised her with an unusual gift at her graduation party. The parents had contacted her school friends before the party and videotaped each of them telling a unique but true story about the graduate.

Each guest was asked to come dressed as a kindergartner with ruffly dresses or short pants, hair bows, or slicked-down hair, and lollipops. The games were all little-kid games such as "Mother, May I" or "Simon Says."

The lunch consisted entirely of finger foods: chicken legs, potato sticks, carrot strips, grapes, and cupcakes. As the cupcakes were served, the tape was played amid groans and laughter over the stories.

A FLOWERY BRIDAL SHOWER

This beautiful and entertaining bridal shower focuses on a garden theme with a wishing well. Construct a full-size wishing well from cardboard and cover it with stone or brick-patterned paper. With a staple gun, the work goes fast and it delivers a unique impact. Decorate the roof and sides with artificial flowers and greenery.

As guests arrive, their shower gifts are placed in the well until time to be opened. Fresh flowers on the tables and floral-designed plates, cups, and paper napkins continue the floral theme.

Play the "flowery" game that ties in with the theme. Give each guest a copy of the list of numbered flowers, some of which will be answers to the questions. See page 118.

ANNIVERSARIES FROM ONE TO SIXTY

Many anniversary parties are built around gifts—the so-called recommended gifts designated for each year. Here's a modern list:

1. Paper	8. Games	35. Coral
2. Cotton	9. Pottery	40. Ruby
3. Plastic	10. Sports	45. Sapphire
4. Linens	15. Crystal	50. Gold
5. Wood	20. China	55. Emerald
6. Plants	25. Silver	60. Diamond
7. Copper, metals	30. Pearl	

Alternate Gift Ideas. You can use this list as a basis for a party theme and gifts, but the longer a couple has been married, the fewer things they need. For celebrating thirty or more years of marriage, *one* item from *all* the guests can be meaningful: a gift of a memory book. In advance, guests send a short write-up of a shared occasion and a significant photo. The hostess then can easily assemble the book before the party. If there is time, it can be enjoyable to read these messages aloud at the party.

Toasts and Roasts. One host asked each invitee to come prepared to give a toast or a roast to the anniversary couple. These provided both laughter and tears of happiness.

THE FLOWERY GAME

Possible answers: (1) Rose (2) Tulips (3) Sweet William (4) Aster (5) Mum (6) Pansy (7) Johnny jump-up (8) Daisy (9) Violet (10) Black-eyed Susan (11) Geranium (12) Daffodil (13) Morning glory (14) Jonquil (15) Lily of the valley (16) Orchid (17) Lady's slipper (18) Bachelor's button (19) Petunia (20) Forget-me-not (21) Poppy (22) Bridal wreath (23) Bluebell (24) Bleeding heart (25) Phlox (26) Four o'clock (27) Iris (28) Jack-in-the-pulpit (29) Sweet peas (30) Sunflower.

Questions:

Example: What did the guests do when the bride started down the aisle? Answer: (1) Rose

1. What was the bridegroom's name?
2. What was the bride's name?
3. How did their wedding day begin?
4. At what hour was the ceremony performed?
5. Who married them?
6. What was the name of the brunette bridesmaid?
7. Which bridesmaid came from between the mountains?
8. Who gave the bride away?
9. What did the bride wear on her head?
10. What did she wear on her feet?
11. Who cried the most at the ceremony?
12. How did she know the groom wanted her?
13. What did the groom see in the bride's eyes?
14. In the reception line, how were the bride and groom greeted?
15. Who was the most melancholy guest?
16. What did the saddest guest have?
17. What flower did the groom remove forever from his buttonhole?
18. What was served at the bridal dinner?
19. What were the groom's parting words to his friends?
20. How many were at the wedding?

Answers: (1) Sweet William (2) Violet or Daisy (3) Morning glory (4) Four-o'clock (5) Jack-in-the-pulpit (6) Black-eyed Susan (7) Lily of the valley (8) Poppy (9) Bridal wreath (10) Lady's-slipper (11) Mum (12) Aster (13) Iris (14) Tulips (15) Bluebell (16) Bleeding heart (17) Bachelor's-button (18) Sweet peas (19) Forget-me-not (20) Phlox

From *The Family Party Book*, copyright © 1996 by Caryl Krueger

Larger Than Life. At another celebration, the party-givers obtained old photos of the honorees and had them enlarged to poster size. These decorated the walls of the hall where the reception was given.

Anniversary Mixer. Each guest has a card pinned on his back. On it is a scrambled word relating to love and marriage. Guests are given papers with a list of all present. They have to find each person and then write the unscrambled word opposite that person's name. For example, the word EVOL unscrambles to LOVE. Another, FINDERS, unscrambles to FRIENDS. Here are some words you can easily scramble yourself: wedding, commitment, family, children, anniversary, vows, kiss, prayer, bridegroom, hugs, flowers, couple, ring, caring, honesty, home, church, bills, fun.

Let Them Eat Cake. The food at an anniversary celebration doesn't have to be a formal meal. A casual afternoon open house works nicely. One event for about fifty friends featured a buffet table with eight different flavors of cakes plus toppings such as fudge sauce, whipped cream, custard, and diced fruit. Guests were given dinner-size plates to hold their creative concoctions.

BABY SHOWER MERRIMENT

No longer are these events restricted to women—some of the best baby showers include the prospective dads. These suggestions work well for either kind of party.

The Tasting Game. You'll need twelve jars of baby food and a number of small disposable spoons (twelve times the number of guests). Take the labels off the baby foods, but number each jar and keep a list of the number and contents. The jars should be: carrots, squash, sweet potatoes, peaches, apricots, bananas, applesauce, beets, prunes, plums, beans, peas. Each guest is given a list numbered from one to twelve, and takes a single taste from each jar in order to try identifying it. This game lets parents know why babies make those faces when being fed!

The game can also be played a harder way—by just trying to identify the foods visually. That's why it's important to have several in the same orange, red, or green colors.

The Advice Game. Prepare a list of problem situations that require parental attention, writing each one on the top half of a piece of paper. Give one to each guest and ask him to write the proper advice or solution on the bottom half of the page. Collect these and cut them in half, giving the top halves to the prospective parent and putting the bottom halves in a bowl. Have the parent-to-be take one of the problem situations and draw one of the advice solutions from the bowl—and then read them together as one sentence. The mismatched combinations can be quite funny.

Here are some situations: If the baby cries you should . . . When the diaper is wet, the first thing you should do is . . . When the baby is teething, remember to . . .

Should the baby get diaper rash, you should . . . If the baby gets hiccups, always . . . At two in the morning when the baby cries, get up and . . . When you take baby for a walk in the stroller, you should . . . If you are going to have your mother baby-sit, be sure to . . . If you are going to have your mother-in-law baby-sit, be sure to . . . While feeding the baby with a tiny spoon, it is essential to . . . When the baby spits up, be sure to . . . When a baby is playing with a rattle . . . If a husband tries to help with the baby, you should . . . To properly burp a baby, first . . . So as to avoid a leaky diaper, remember to . . . When taking the baby's temperature, it's essential to . . . While bathing a baby, it's fun to . . . As you sing a lullaby to the baby, also . . .

Who's That Cute Baby? Ask guests to bring baby pictures of themselves. Number them and pin them on the walls of the party room. Give guests numbered papers and see who can correctly identify the most babies.

A Funny Thing Happened. So often friends share horror stories with parents-to-be. Instead, have guests share the most amusing or heartwarming things that have happened to them and their child.

After the Baby Shower. For a first baby, it's fun to have a shower before the baby is born since the parents will need many things. But for subsequent babies, the needs differ. Tell the parents you want to have a shower *after* the little one is born. Plan it as a dinner at their house, but bring all the food and beverages, enough so that there will be plenty of leftovers, and also the linens, decorations, or flowers. Tell guests the baby's name in advance so that there can be gender-correct gifts. Afterwards, be sure to tidy up so that the parents have no work at all.

New Mom's Day. Instead of gifts for the baby, gift an after-the-birth shower for the mother. Plan it to begin at baby's afternoon naptime. First, serve a lunch completely prepared by the guests and then let the mother nap as the group prepares dinner and tidies the house.

When the mother awakens, treat her to an at-home manicure, pedicure, facial, massage, hair cut—whatever talents the group has or can afford to hire for care at home. Then present her with a group gift of something new to wear (purchased at a store where it can be exchanged if needed).

When baby wakes up, admire the little person and take turns at holding, set the dinner table for two, and leave the house looking neat.

Casserole Shower. Instead of a gift, each guest brings a written promise of a casserole or dinner she or he will prepare and bring to the new parents after baby's arrival. (This can be varied by promising errand-running, baby-sitting, manicure, staying over and taking the night feedings, or other helpful services.) The promises are redeemed by the parents by giving a forty-eight hour notice.

BON VOYAGE PARTY

Whether friends are leaving for a trip, or moving to a new city, you can make their departure festive and memorable.

Bon Voyage for a Vacation. If they're going on a cruise, plan a party where guests wear cruise clothes. Have each one bring a small, inexpensive travel essential as a gift. Let the food be an elegant shipboard buffet complete with an ice sculpture (kitchen shops have ice molds).

Since bingo and shuffleboard are favorite shipboard games, play those and give prizes—tickets to local attractions for the stay-at-homes.

Bon Voyage When Friends Are Moving. If your party honors someone moving away from the area, give them something to remember you by—something that can be made in advance or right at the party.

Buy a tablecloth and eight napkins and provide contrasting embroidery thread and several needles. All guests (yes, men are good at this too) stitch their names on the cloth (around the edge) or on the corner of a napkin.

An alternate idea begins with a large ceramic plate, paint, and glaze purchased at a do-it-yourself pottery shop. In advance, arrange to have all the guests sign the plate. (If this isn't possible, you can letter all the names on the plate.) Then, you apply the glaze and take the plate back to the pottery shop to be fired as a permanent memento.

Photos. For bon voyage parties of all types, photographs are essential. If friends are moving away, consider taking Polaroid pictures and making an album at the party, providing a place for each guest to write a farewell message.

NO-WATCH RETIREMENT PARTY

No gold watches are permitted at this party! Instead, have a roast with funny toasts and speeches given in honor of the retiree. Gifts can be equipment needed for retirement: senior discount cards, passes to a movie theater, local bus tickets, sunglasses or visors and sunscreen lotion, board games and decks of cards, sports equipment, a jump rope and set of weights, the start of a collection, books, and audio cassettes.

If the retiree has won awards or had her picture in publications, make a display of these for all to admire.

Play the fill-in-the-blank story game (see page 87, making up a story about the guest of honor's past and future life.)

One innovative party-giver honored retirement and antiquity by asking each guest to bring for show-and-tell the oldest thing they had in their own home. This made everyone feel very young!

THE ACADEMY AWARD CELEBRITY PARTY

Make Oscar night a personal triumph with a party of your movie-going friends on Academy Awards night. Older youngsters like this party, too. When extending the invitations, encourage guests to see as many of the contending films as possible. If you and your friends enjoy dressing up, have them come in formal wear or costumed as a favorite star.

As guests gather, provide a buffet of foods easily eaten on TV tables or lap trays in front of the television. At commercial breaks, encourage everyone to serve themselves and return to a different seat.

Before the TV show begins, give each guest a ballot to mark with their choices of winners. They should put their own name on the ballot. (You can make your own ballot or use the list usually found in the newspaper a few weeks before the event.) Then exchange ballots so that another person will be awarding the points for correct answers.

As each award is given, announce the number of points for a correct guess. (Technical awards—one point; makeup—two points; cinematography—three points; costume awards—four points; writing awards—five points; music awards—six points; foreign films—seven points; supporting actor/actress—eight points each; best director—nine points; best picture, best actress, best actor—ten points each.)

At the end of the evening, each ballot is totaled and the top winners are given movie passes (available at your local theater).

THE POLITICALLY CORRECT PARTY

This party is ideal for Election Day evening or on Inauguration Day morning. Guests are encouraged to give their personal ideas on politicians, the country's needs, and on good government—or bad.

If the party is held on election night, start with dessert around 8 P.M. As results come in, let guests predict how they think the election will affect your town, state, or the nation.

For an Inauguration Day party, you may want to serve breakfast before watching the ceremonies. However, since this is a work day, you can tape the inauguration and hold the party in the evening.

Make name tags for all political posts: President, Vice President, Speaker, Secretaries of State/Defense/Education, Governor, Mayor, Senator, Congressman, and so on. As guests arrive, let each choose what office he or she would like to hold and wear that tag.

When ceremony viewing ends, each guest takes on the persona of his chosen politician and tells what he hopes to accomplish during his term. And depending on the political affiliation of the guest, this will be both serious and fun.

Since politicians are known for their doublespeak, let guests translate the following sentences into their well-known everyday sayings. You can either divide guests into two teams and then read the double-talk statements (giving a point for the first team to correctly answer) or you can copy the double-talk statements page and let guests work with pencils to translate them. (See "No More Doublespeak" on following page.)

STREET PARTY

It's enjoyable to gather neighbors together once each year and many residents of blocks, buildings, or neighborhoods appreciate an event that brings them closer together on a social basis. A good time for this party is at the end of summer when people have returned from vacations and kids will soon be going back to school. These activities work well when held at a house with a large yard or at a nearby park:

1. **Just Ten.** Guests are invited to bring a ten minute video, ten slides, or ten photos from their travels or home activities. It's fun to see where everyone has been or what they've been doing.

2. **Backyard Potluck.** Encourage neighbors to bring a casserole, salad and rolls, or dessert to share. Also, lawn chairs and sports equipment. Many neighborhoods make this a cookout with each family bringing their own meat, and the host families or a committee providing the trimmings.

3. **Water Targets.** With string or chalk, make a circle ten feet in diameter on the grass. Three adults (in rainwear) volunteer to be targets in the center of the circle. Place pails of water around the circle and provide sponges for throwing. No winners, no losers, just wet hilarious fun.

4. **Adults as Kids.** Play two-generation kid games with adults participating: tag, hide-and-seek, hopscotch (especially good), a slip and slide, croquet, beanbag toss. Adults and kids can also play together on swings and slides.

5. **Target Practice.** Use string to hang many targets (aluminum pie pans are

NO MORE DOUBLESPEAK!

1. Scintillate, scintillate mini-asteroid.

2. Members of an avian species of identical plumage congregate.

3. Surveillance should precede gigantic movement.

4. It is fruitless to weep about an overturned lactose product.

5. Freedom from incrustations of grime must precede a holy state.

6. The writing implement is more potent than the cutlass.

7. It is futile to attempt to indoctrinate an aged canine with innovative maneuvers.

8. Forsake the implement of correction and impair the offspring.

9. The temperature of the aqueous content of a saucepan unremittingly observed does not reach 212 degrees Fahrenheit.

10. Every article that lustrously glows, is not truly auriferous.

11. When there are visible vapors of carbonaceous materials, there is conflagration.

12. Moochers are not permitted to select.

13. A plethora of individuals with culinary skills bring about contamination of the porridge.

14. Loving deeds have their initial action under one's own roof.

15. Male cadavers are incapable of yielding testimony.

16. Individuals who make their abode in vitreous edifices would be well-advised to refrain from catapulting projectiles.

17. Exclusive dedication to chores without interludes of hedonistic diversion renders John a lackluster fellow.

18. Revolving mineral matter accumulates no small, green bryophytic plant.

19. Attractiveness achieves solely epidermis extent.

20. Missiles of twigs or rock have the potential of fracturing osseous structures, but utterance will eternally remain innocuous.

1. Twinkle, twinkle, little star. 2. Birds of a feather stick together. 3. Look before you leap 4. Don't cry over spilt milk. 5. Cleanliness comes before godliness. 6. The pen is mightier than the sword. 7. You can't teach an old dog new tricks. 8. Spare the rod and spoil the child. 9. The watched pot never boils. 10. All that glitters is not gold. 11. Where there's smoke, there's fire. 12. Beggars can't be choosers. 13. Too many cooks spoil the soup. 14. Charity begins at home. 15. Dead men can't talk. 16. People who live in glass houses shouldn't throw stones. 17. All work and no play makes Jack a dull boy. 18. A rolling stone gathers no moss. 19. Beauty is only skin deep. 20. Sticks and stones may break my bones but words can never hurt me.

excellent) from a tree branch or a rope between two posts. Using tennis balls, participants get three tries to hit a target. Provide a candy reward for good aim.

6. **Weight Guessing.** Let one adult be the official guesser as willing neighbors step on the scale. Give a snack or beverage prize to those who fool the guesser by more than five pounds.

7. **Cracker Whistling.** How fast can you give a real whistle with a mouthful of crackers? Use a stopwatch as each contestant puts two crackers in his mouth and then tries to whistle. Shortest time wins.

8. **Cherry Twist.** While there are a very few people who can tie a knot in a cherry stem inside their mouths, here's a cute way to surprise everyone with this skill. The trickster goes to get a big bowl of cherries, and while away from the group, he takes a stem, ties it in a knot, and places it in his cheek. Another person, in on the secret, gives each person a cherry on a stem and tells them to save the cherry for later eating, but to put the stem in their mouth and tie it in a knot. The trickster pretends to go along with this and contorts his mouth and lips as if really working hard to do this. Time is called after two minutes and only the trickster will have achieved success.

Along with the fun, this street party is also an excellent time to discuss neighborhood safety, the importance of a neighborhood watch organization, and to identify those families who have children home alone after school.

A PARTY WITH CHURCH FRIENDS

Partying with those who attend church or synagogue with you gives an added dimension to fellowship.

Eating in the Garden of Eden. Have a dinner where each invitee brings a food mentioned in the Bible (be sure to include Eve's apples). The host family prepares a leg-of-lamb while the others furnish corn, bread, wine, grape salad, cake, and so forth.

Bible Charades. For hilarious fun, organize charades by giving out Bible story titles to pairs to act out, or just let people volunteer when they think of one. Of course, no words can be used, but lots of posing and movement will help define the subject.

Consider these: the serpent offering the apple to Eve, the boys in the fiery furnace, Moses parting the sea, Jesus walking on water, Naomi following Ruth, the three wisemen, David defeating Goliath, casting pearls before swine, Jesus turning water into wine, Paul being bitten by the viper, Daniel in the lion's den, Jesus feeding the multitude, eating sour grapes and the child's teeth being set on edge, Jonah and the whale, Noah's ark. (This last one was performed by three pairs of people pretending to be long-necked giraffes, hopping rabbits, and elephants with trunks, being led by Noah. It was the grand finale!)

Find the Books. This game works well with folks who know the names of the books of the Bible. Fifteen book names are hidden in this story: (Make a copy for each player.)

THE HIDDEN BOOKS OF THE BIBLE

I once made a remark about the hidden books of the Bible. It was a lulu, kept people looking so hard for facts, and for others it was a revelation. Some were in a jam, especially since the names of the books were not capitalized, but the truth finally struck home to numbers of readers. To others, it was a real job. We want it to be a fascinating few moments for you. Yes, there will be some really easy ones to spot. Others may require judges to help them. I will quickly admit it usually takes a minister to find one of them, and there will be loud lamentations when it is found. A little lady says she brews a cup of tea so she can concentrate better. See how well you can compete. Relax now, for there really are fifteen names of the Bible in this story.

1. _____   2. _____   3. _____

4. _____   5. _____   6. _____

7. _____   8. _____   9. _____

10. _____   11. _____   12. _____

13. _____   14. _____   15. _____

(Books, in order: Mark, Luke, Kings, Acts, Revelation, James, Ruth, Numbers, Job, Esther, Judges, Titus, Lamentations, Hebrews, Peter.)

A CULINARY-JUDGING PARTY

Here's a party I gave because I love to cook and try new recipes. It requires leisurely time to enjoy this meal served to about ten or more good, honest friends. Since almost everyone likes sharing an opinion, this party gives guests the opportunity to state their views on the food.

But before eating, play this game in the kitchen. (Make sure that all items are in view before letting guests into the kitchen to search for them. Copy this list for each player and allow about ten minutes for play:

KITCHEN HIDE-AND-SEEK

1. Dental work
2. Common sense:
3. End of a brief malady:
4. What lovers do:
5. Charge of the light brigade:
6. The lost chord:
7. Under cover:
8. A commentator:
9. Things to adore:
10. Switch tender:
11. When amazed, you're:
12. An absorbing subject:
13. Sad end of a ship:
14. Event at the start of a party:
15. Cowboy's territory:
16. Insincere flattery:
17. Peacemakers:
18. Medieval form of torture:
19. A yenta's job:
20. Critics do it:

Answers: 1. plate 2. pennies 3. cup (hiccup) 4. spoon 5. electric bill 6. string, cord 7. table with cloth on it 8. potato 9. keys 10. hairpin 11. floored 12. sponge 13. sink 14. mixer 15. range 16. soft soap 17. scissors 18. rack 19. matches 20. pan

From *The Family Party Book*, copyright © 1996 by Caryl Krueger

Here are the recipes I tried at a luncheon party with fifteen women bridge friends. It was fun to hear their frank remarks about my cooking! Following appetizers, I served a buffet luncheon with five new-to-me salads, served with two kinds of hot breads. Three of the salads got unanimous raves and all salads passed muster—although there were some friendly arguments when one guest would say *marvelous* and another would answer *just so-so*.

While you can have a food-judging party with many different menus, here are the five salads I chose to serve:

1. Heavenly Ham Salad

> 1 pound boneless ham, ground in food processor
> ¼ cup peanut butter
> 3 tablespoons lime (or lemon) juice
> 1 teaspoon ground ginger
> 1 clove garlic, minced
> ½ red onion minced
> ¾ cup celery, diced
> ¼ cup non-fat sour cream
> ¼ cup fat-free mayonnaise or salad dressing

In a large bowl, mix all ingredients, except the last two, until well-blended. Then add sour cream and mayonnaise to desired consistency and refrigerate until served.

2. Peppy Pea Salad

> 3 packages (10 ounces each) frozen petite peas, thawed
> ½ cup green olives, sliced
> ½ cup celery thinly sliced
> 1 small onion finely chopped
> ¼ pound mushrooms, thinly sliced
> 6 slices bacon
> ½ cup mayonnaise
> ½ cup sour cream
> 2½ tablespoons cider or white wine vinegar
> ½ teaspoon dry tarragon
> ½ teaspoon ground nutmeg
> 2 tablespoons Dijon mustard

In a large bowl, mix together mayonnaise, sour cream, vinegar, tarragon, nutmeg, and mustard. You can set aside or store dressing at this point. In a frying pan, cook bacon until crisp, then drain and crumble. Using 3 tablespoons of the drippings, add onion and cook, stirring occasionally, until limp. Add mushrooms, stirring occasionally until soft. Remove from heat and add celery and olives. You can set aside or store vegetables at this point. Prior to serving, mix peas with vegetables and bacon, then add dressing mixture.

3. **Exotic Fruit Salad**

Romaine lettuce leaves
4 oranges, peeled, cut in half, sliced
1 pound fresh figs, cut into 8 slices each
½ pound dates, pitted and diced
3 kiwi fruit, sliced
½ cup orange juice
¼ cup cider vinegar
2 tablespoons olive oil
2 tablespoons honey
1 tablespoon grated orange rind
¼ teaspoon salt

In a large bowl, mix four fruits together. Place remaining six ingredients in a jar and shake vigorously. Gently mix dressing with fruit. Arrange lettuce in a bowl, add salad and serve.

4. **Savory Pasta Salad**

16 ounces pasta
1 teaspoon salt
1 tablespoon oil
2 cups of broccoli florets, no stems
3 carrots peeled and sliced on the diagonal
1 bunch scallions with tops, sliced on the diagonal
½ pound snow peas
1 red pepper, cored and seeded
1 yellow pepper, cored and seeded
4 cooked chicken breasts, diced

Cut the six vegetables into bite size pieces and blanch until tender-crisp. Cook pasta in boiling water with salt and oil, cooking for ten minutes until al dente, then drain, rinse, and place in a large bowl. Toss with one-fourth of the salad dressing (recipe follows). When pasta is cool, toss with all remaining ingredients and chill until ready to serve. At serving time, toss with the remaining dressing.

Dressing: Mix all ingredients in a blender until smooth:

¾ cup rice vinegar
¼ cup soy sauce
3 tablespoons vegetable oil
2 teaspoons sesame oil
⅓ cup peanut butter
1 tablespoon sugar

2 teaspoons grated ginger
2 teaspoons dry mustard
3 teaspoons crushed garlic

129

5. Orange-Potato Salad

No one will recognize the orange in this salad, yet it adds a special tang.

> 2 pounds cooked russet potatoes, cooled, peeled and cut into half-inch chunks
> 2 oranges, peeled, membrane removed, and cut into segments
> ½ cup diced cheddar cheese
> 3 teaspoons grated orange rind
> ¼ cup orange juice
> ¼ cup grated parmesan cheese
> ½ cup packed fresh parsley
> ½ cup packed fresh cilantro (coriander)
> 1 cup unflavored yogurt
> 1 teaspoon brown sugar
> ½ cup pecan pieces
> Salt and pepper to taste

In a food processor, blend orange rind, orange juice, parmesan cheese, parsley, cilantro, yogurt, and brown sugar. In a large bowl, mix potato cubes, orange segments, and diced cheddar cheese. Chill together and add seasoning to taste. Add pecan pieces just before serving.

* * *

From these ideas, you can see that you needn't wait for Dad's birthday or New Year's Eve in order to entertain. There are many unique create-your-own party ideas just waiting for you and your friends to enjoy.

Memorable Reunions Without Struggle

Reunions can be some of the most memorable events in anyone's life. Reunions let the participants look both backward and forward and emphasize the high points in their lives. While this chapter focuses on family reunions, many of these ideas can also be used for school reunions and less elaborate family get-togethers.

If you have not been part of a reunion, start planning one now. If you've already had one, read on for new ideas for your next one.

WHY A REUNION?

The reasons for getting together can vary just as reunions vary in their style. Your reunion might be as small as a dozen people or it can consist of a clan of hundreds. Some reunions offer just one meal and conversation—others consist of an entire week of activities. Some are a once-in-a-lifetime experience, others are held yearly. Some are a potluck in the park, others take place on elegant cruise ships. But remember that whatever you plan, make it unique while not making it a chore. It will require work, but it doesn't have to be a struggle. The easier way is often the better way!

Many reunions commemorate past history, such as graduations or military service, while others celebrate wedding anniversaries or very special birthdays. Yet, you don't have to honor a particular event to have a reunion; instead you can make the focus a simple gathering of relatives or good friends. No matter what category your reunion falls into, you'll follow many of the same planning steps.

First, you need to assess the interest in a get-together. For a school reunion, you'll send a brief inquiry asking if the classmates would come to a reunion (name the year, month, and place). For a family party, you can simply confer with a few key relatives. Don't be concerned if some people say they won't take part—that's their loss!

Your vital interest in sharing fellowship is reason enough for a reunion.

GETTING ORGANIZED

Depending on the size of your reunion, you'll need one well-organized person or a committee to carry out the special duties. The head person is usually called The Coordinator. (Now that title doesn't mean you have to do it all unless you really want to!)

The Coordinator can be the sole organizer if the reunion is to be for twenty or fewer people. (Actually this is fine since you get to make all the decisions!) But the moment the party passes the twenty person mark, you'll probably welcome the help of others. These are some of the other committee posts needed, depending on your planned activities, the number attending, and the duration of the event:

1. Communications Chairperson. This should be a person who has a computer and is willing to send out four or five mailings, plus keeping a list of information on those attending.
2. Finance Chairperson. Mailings, meals, souvenirs, prizes, housing, can cost real money. Most every sizable reunion, whether for schoolmates or relatives, charges a suitable fee that will cover expenses but not discourage possible attenders.
3. Food Chairperson. Some reunions have only one meal, usually a potluck. Still, someone has to assign the food, get the supplies, arrange it on the buffet, organize the cleanup. Larger reunions may require someone to make arrangements with restaurants for catered meals and a final banquet.
4. Activities Chairperson. This is your most creative committee member—one who can bring the group together for both fellowship and fun. Duties include the selection of people to honor, games to play, group excursions, and so forth.
5. Kids' Activities Chairperson. If there will be many children present, you'll want to have some activities especially geared for them. This chair will have to find or provide entertainment, games, and caregivers to oversee the activities.
6. Housing Chairperson. Where to put everyone staying overnight can take some effort. This post should be handled by someone who is good at arrangements and negotiation.

All of these aspects of the reunion are fully explained in this chapter and you'll see how stress-free—and satisfying—reunion planning can be.

CHOOSING THE DATE

It sounds far away, but pick a date at least a year in advance—forewarning will result in the best attendance. If the reunion commemorates a special happening (such as a golden anniversary or an eightieth birthday), pick a date as close to that event as possible. Either check the chosen date with the honorees or, if it's to be a surprise, arrange with a family member to see that they reserve the time for some trumped-up event.

Good weather is an advantage, especially if there will be outdoor events. Thus, popular times for reunions are holidays (Memorial Day, Independence Day, Labor Day) where there are three-day weekends and the likelihood of fair weather.

Also popular is the long Thanksgiving Day weekend, which allows distant relatives time to travel. Because holidays are busy travel times, it is absolutely necessary to make airline and other reservations well in advance.

But don't rule out a winter reunion date. In some areas, there are great bargains in the winter. And for many, a winter trip to a warm climate, or a resort with a pool, can be a real drawing card. For others, a cozy lodge in the mountains near hiking and skiing is ideal.

For a reunion that includes youngsters, choose a date that ties in with school vacation days.

Making the date known a year or more ahead is your number one priority.

SELECTING THE PLACE AND LODGINGS

The site can be a simple decision or a major negotiation. For a one-meal or one-day reunion, a park, a private room at a restaurant, or your own large backyard can be ideal. But when attenders are coming a long distance, you will probably need a meeting place suitable for several days of activities.

For a family reunion, the family farm or accommodations in the original hometown add a wonderful historical aura to the event. Returning to one's roots can be nostalgic and memorable.

Many successful reunions are held at a campground. Tents and sleeping bags, motor homes and trailers, or rented cabins, combined with potlucks and cookouts plus homemade games, can certainly keep the costs down and provide many days of fun. Off-season rates can make these locations even more attractive.

A piece of advice: should you choose an outdoor location, have a back-up site in case of bad weather. Talk to your church or club about the possibility of using a room there in case the weatherman surprises you with a July 4th thunderstorm!

One family holds a yearly reunion hosted by the grandparents who choose a sports-oriented location, such as a national park or rustic resort, and pay for the accommodations. The week-long event is comprised mostly of outdoor activities with various pairings among siblings and relatives with similar interests such as kayaking, sailing, fishing, rafting, or hiking. Adults take turns at being "Kid

Koordinator" for a day or evening and arrange and oversee activities just for the young. Dinners are eaten together and evenings are spent with games and home-grown entertainment.

When a number of relatives live in one area, they can often house the out-of-towners. And sometimes your good friends may be willing to house your relatives. If this is the plan, be sure you make very definite arrangements with the guests as to their hosts' mealtimes, keys, parking, laundry, and quiet hours. And remind them to leave the guest quarters neat. (That way your friends may offer to help you another time.)

One large house can also provide accommodations for a small reunion and this has the advantage of having everyone under one roof. With cots and sleeping bags to supplement the bedrooms, you can create great camaraderie since you will be sharing common areas, bathrooms, and kitchen.

For large reunions, hotel/motel accommodations may be the answer—sometimes just for night-time lodging, sometimes as the actual site of the reunion. There are advantages to this since the hotel staff will do much of the work for you. For a minimum number of rooms reserved, they often throw in a hospitality room that you can use, too.

At many promotion-minded hotels, you can get freebies such as breakfast, airport transportation, an indoor meeting room, evening entertainment, and sports areas such as a pool, tennis courts, or a workout room. Some also provide complimentary newspapers and snacks, discount tickets to local attractions, and free maps and other promotional literature.

Hotel chains in or near major cities offer some of the best deals for the money. You'll want to call and compare prices and features. Here are some suggestions:

Ramada Inns, 800-848-9779 (ask about special Florida reunions)
Best Western, 800-334-7234 (ask for reunion plans)
Holiday Inn, 800-633-8464 or 800-447-7300 (for a free reunion planning guide)

Of course there are accommodations near theme parks and historical sites that can help to make your reunion unique. One family with three generations, the youngest child being age ten, has found that three-day cruises are a good buy since absolutely everything is included in a safe and relaxed environment.

But most reunions will be simple one- to three-day events and you'll need a minimum amount of professional help. For our family reunions, I've found a nearby suburban motel that offers rooms that sleep four, free breakfast, an exercise room, and a pool for only forty-five dollars a day. On Georgia's ocean front, you can stay at an inn with many perks for forty dollars per room. Across the country at a resort on San Diego's Mission Bay, you get free airport pick up, health club, tennis and racquetball, and hospitality room for get-togethers, all for sixty-five dollars per room.

Your Automobile Club can also help you find the ideal place that also meets your budget.

Knowing the interests of the people coming to the reunion, as well as their financial abilities, will help you choose the perfect location, whether it's a park or palace.

SET THE THEME

A first reunion may not require a theme, but if you plan to get together with some regularity, it's intriguing to have a different theme each time.

A year-of-graduation-from-school reunion can use the date as the theme and ask invitees to dress as they did that year.

Ethnicity can also be a theme. One family of German descent uses their ancestors' traditional ways as a theme, and the dessert for every reunion is a delicious apple concoction called apfelkuchen.

Other themes can tie in with the holidays. A Fourth of July chili cook-off, a Christmas-in-June theme, or a Thanksgiving reunion that features the turkey feast one day, turkey sandwiches the next, then turkey tacos, and finally turkey hash.

From my survey, other successful reunions have been built around a wild west theme, a Polynesian luau, Mickey Mouse and a trip to Disneyland, or a black-tie formal banquet. One large reunion features a time capsule (see chapter 3 for a description of a time capsule party) and a meeting every decade. Another family finds that it's easy to remember their reunions since they get together in years ending in the numbers zero and five.

But don't feel pressured to have a theme: Creative planning combined with attention-to-detail can make any reunion good fellowship.

WHOM TO INVITE

Let your motto for invitations be inclusive rather than exclusive. Forget about family feuds—most people behave acceptably when in a group or when watchful youngsters are on hand! Invitees with problems (diffidence, combativeness, senility, alcoholism, violence) should have a caretaker specifically assigned to oversee their participation.

While school or military reunions have a set list, family reunions can expand to include relatives of relatives and even those special friends who are just like relatives. Your best source of names will be the person who acts as family genealogist or an older family member who regularly keeps in touch with everyone.

If you are serious about finding long-lost relatives, you can trace your roots with help from the National Genealogical Society, 4527 17th Street North, Arlington, VA 22207-2399, phone: 703-525-0050.

As your invitation list grows, put it on computer or make an index card for each person, couple, or family. Include name, address, phone, ages, occupations, hobbies, and talents.

These records are essential to the success of your current reunion and invaluable research for future get-togethers.

WHO PAYS WHAT

We would all like an angel—dear grandparents who treat everyone to a reunion at a fabulous resort—but that doesn't often happen. When a reunion is a one-day event at a large home or in the park, the cost is sometimes borne by one family, with the hope that another family will do it another year. But far more common is the reunion where the costs are shared.

It's usually up to attenders to pay for their own transportation to the event and for meals not provided at the reunion.

The Coordinator (or committee) can determine the other costs and charge a reunion fee, usually on a per adult basis, with youngsters under eighteen at half-price. Although teens can eat just as much as adults, the half-price encourages entire families to attend, and they are often the backbone of much of the fun.

The reunion fee should cover invitations, other mailings and postage, printing/copying, long-distance phone calls, the meals eaten together, name tags and paper supplies, rentals, flowers and decorations, entertainment/musicians, games, and prizes. If possible, it can also cover a hired photographer and one group photo per family, the family history book, T-shirts, or other memorabilia.

One large family includes in the reunion fee a small sum for an educational grant. Each year the committee honors those youngsters starting college with a small monetary award.

So as to enable as many as possible to attend, keep the costs—and thus the reunion fee—as low as possible.

PROMOTING THE REUNION

Selling the reunion—making it sound like an event that must not be missed—is the object of your promotion. Of course you can do it by phone, fax, or E-mail, but an intriguing mailed invitation will bring the best response. (The timetable at the end of this chapter will give you added information.)

The First Mailing. When you have consulted with the group or your committee and have a date and place, send your first announcement. Give the specifics and enclose a stamped postcard for response, asking that it be returned by a specific date. (Don't then immediately take nonresponders off your list, as they may just be slow in answering due to a vacation, busyness, or lack of social skills.)
Enclose sparkle confetti (available at a party shop) in the envelope of this first letter, and in with your sincere invitation for them to come, give some of the highlights of the event. On the return card, ask for pertinent information such as possibility of attending, names of others who should be invited, what help or talent can be offered.

Monthly Newsletter. Some large reunion groups then continue with a monthly newsletter about the reunion, but most family reunions use about four more mailings after the initial invitation.

Second Mailing. Your next communication (about nine months ahead) will be more detailed, specifying the reunion fee, deadline for reservations, and providing more program information. At this point, be sure to ask for names and ages of youngsters attending.

Third and Fourth Mailings. At both the six- and three-month points, you will continue to promote with names of folks who are coming, events to be held, and specific things to bring, such as family photo albums and other memorabilia.

Final Reminder. An important communication is the one sent three to four weeks in advance. This is a reminder with updated information, plus a list of things to bring (such as contributions to the potluck, photos, games or sports equipment, flashlight—if at a campsite, special clothes) as well as a map showing the location, other travel and pick-up arrangements, lodging confirmation, and expected weather.

In your communications, be very accurate. Include easy-to-read lists: who is coming, what to bring, planned events. Make your wording so intriguing that invitees will be eager to come.

FEEDING THE CROWD

A meal for a multitude is a great mixer for several generations of families. But making provisions for meals varies considerably depending on your event.

If you're at a hotel or resort, all of your meals may be supplied. Or, for some meals, guests will be on their own and would welcome a list of suggested eateries. A nostalgic meal at a college reunion can be eaten in the campus dining room or an off-campus spot that was a favorite in past times.

At a park or campsite with cooking and eating facilities, you may provide some of the meals, and guests will supply others. Families can eat their breakfasts on their own. Sandwiches, chips, fruit, and sodas can be set out for an easy-to-prepare lunch. Then, each night, one or two families can host the supper, importing the food, doing the cooking and cleanup, or treating the group to a restaurant meal.

Plan to serve family favorites, especially ethnic dishes, and have kid-tested foods available for the littlest fingers. And be sure the men cook, too. For one family that has a yearly reunion in cabins on a lake, the Sunday morning pancake breakfast, cooked by the guys with great fanfare and lots of humor, is a highlight.

For many family reunions, the first meal is often a potluck. This means that travelers from afar should be assigned breads, pies or cakes, paper supplies, chips and snacks, beverages, or other nonperishables. The local folk can make the main dish or casserole and the accompanying vegetables and salads. This potluck meal is often the culinary highlight of the event, with everyone interested in the best recipes made by each cook.

A catered dinner is another possibility, especially if the reunion goes on for several days. The Coordinator can check prices of professional catering companies, as well as church auxiliaries who also cater meals.

Since guests don't all arrive at the same moment, appetizers or snacks with punch should be served to ward off hunger pangs. If you plan to serve substantial appetizers at a hotel site, you can cut the cost of the dinner by not having another first course.

For a reunion that lasts more than a day, a final formal banquet is often planned. But to cut costs, the final meal can be a luncheon—or even a generous breakfast— before guests start to return home.

The Coordinator should make a fair plan for the set-up and cleanup of meals, so that these tasks don't fall onto just a few willing souls.

Expensive food and elegant surroundings aren't necessary for a satisfying reunion—it's the shared experience of tasty food and camaraderie that brings people closer together.

THE ALL-IMPORTANT PHOTOGRAPH

Don't leave it to chance that amateur photographers will capture a good shot of Uncle Charlie, or the class valedictorian, or the platoon commander. Hire a professional photographer to be at the main event so that a group photo—one that includes everyone—can be taken, as well as a few other not-to-be-missed photos.

The Coordinator should be empowered to select from the proofs the group photo where most folks look best and order one for each attending family. If the group photo is not included in your reunion fee, have a sign-up sheet for those who wish to order pictures. Ask one person to make the rounds with this sign-up sheet at the main event so that no one misses out.

Beyond that, you can let the amateur photographers take over, with the understanding that good photos will be shared for the reunion scrapbook. Subjects for these pictures should be: the guest of honor, game winners, the emcee in action, oldest and youngest attending, family with most children, family who came the farthest, scenes at events such as dances and storytelling, plus behind-the-scenes shots taken in the kitchen or building the campfire, and sleepyheads nestled in their beds.

When there will be a guest of honor, ask attenders to bring to the event a photo of themselves *with* the honoree. Have a scrapbook, glue, and pens on hand so that each guest can put his picture in the book and write an appropriate message with it, making a long-lasting memento.

SOUVENIRS AND REMEMBRANCES

Souvenirs add spirit to the actual event and these small remembrances bring the good times to mind when the event is over. You may wish to give some of these as gifts or include the purchase of them in the reunion fee.

T-shirts. A large group of people wearing identical shirts can be fun. In a mailing, get the sizes of those coming and order the shirts in advance. They can say "Class of 1960," "Wilton Family Reunion," "Uncle Ralph: 90 and Going Strong," or whatever you like. Prices start at about six dollars for a lightweight adult shirt. Check with your local T-shirt company or get a bid from Reunion Research at 209-855-2101.

Caps. Personalized caps are extremely popular and usually cost about the same as a shirt.

Mugs and Totes. If you'd rather carry a souvenir than wear one, consider personalized backpacks or tote bags, glasses or mugs.

Family Calendar. When attenders sign up for a reunion, have them supply their birth and anniversary dates. Then, prepare a calendar for the following year showing all these dates. Local quick print shops can print one for each family at a reasonable price.

Reunion Calendar. Choose the twelve best photos taken at the reunion. Have these reproduced in calendars for the coming year. Check with various quick print shops for the least expensive price. Certainly have one of these made if there is a guest of honor, or consider sending one to each family.

Memory Book. Assign scribes (from the literate folks attending) to act as reporters and write a brief summary of the events and meals. (We did this on my parents' fiftieth anniversary trip through Scandinavia and the reports done by the grandchildren were far more interesting than the adult write-ups!) Assemble the reports in chronological order and where there are spaces, paste in photos that will copy well. Then make sufficient copies of the pages and gather each set into a colorful binder. Mail this memory book to each family.

Family Cookbook. Everyone will want recipes of the foods served, especially if there's been a potluck. In advance, ask cooks to bring copies of their best family recipes. After the reunion, compile all of these into a small family cookbook. As the years pass and you collect more recipes at each reunion, you may eventually want to make a more professional cookbook. If so, get information from Walter's Cookbooks, 1050 8th Street, N.E., Waseca, MN 56093, Phone: 800-447-3274, Fax 507-835-3217.

Storytelling History Book. At one reunion event (perhaps one evening around a fire), make an audiotape of older family members sharing an oral history. Other favorite or unique family stories can follow. Transcribe the tape (type it out) to make a family history book and be sure to include an up-to-date family tree. Distribute a copy to each family. Collect information at each reunion and send an updated page of the latest news and individual accomplishments to the families involved.

The Video Story. Assign one good videographer to tape reunion highlights from start to finish. Make copies of the video available at cost to interested families.

The Family Quilt. This requires some family members willing to sew and to quilt. At one reunion, have each person bring an eight-by-eight-inch square of their favorite fabric—childhood blanket, prom dress, cozy bathrobe, upholstery fabric, whatever. Then between reunions, the sewers create a family quilt from all the pieces and embroider the person's name on the square. At the next reunion, the quilt is presented and the stories behind the squares are shared. The quilt can be given to the oldest member of the family, or to the guest of honor, or it can be raffled off with the money going toward educational grants for college-bound youths.

ACTIVITIES FOR YOUNG AND OLD

While conversation and sharing of news take up much of the reunion time, other activities should also be planned.

First get-together activities as guests arrive

1. **Name Tags.** At the entry, have a table with prepared name tags for everyone. Make these in advance and put in the middle a word about the person. (Thus, a name tag would read Diane "the equestrian" Barnett, or Joshua "the computer whiz" Garcia.) This small touch creates a topic of conversation as people meet.

2. **Family Tree.** On an easel or wall, display a family tree, showing all family members. Use blue ink for those not present, red for those present. Guests will spend a lot of time looking at it to see how they're related to others.

3. **Photo Board.** On one or more posterboards, affix family photos with easy-to-remove rubber cement. Identify the people in each one. Encourage guests to add more photos and provide a pen to label them.

4. **Photo Album Table.** Provide a table and chairs for viewing family photo albums brought to the event.

5. **Introductions.** With everyone present, the emcee (which might be the coordinator) introduces the guest of honor if there is one, and then the family members starting with the oldest and down to the youngest. The emcee should have an advance guest list so as to be prepared with a comment about each person. Be sure to have a microphone!

6. **Honoring the Guest of Honor.** For this special person, have a unique, large, or decorated chair. For a woman, give a corsage or bouquet, a boutonniere for a man. Encourage adults to give tributes and the kids can read made-in-advance

poems. Present the person with a gift of a flag from his or her ancestral country.

7. **Special Recognition.** Give humorous or appropriate awards to the person who came the farthest (a road map), is oldest or youngest (a box of birthday candles), has the most children (a silver dollar to help pay the bills), graduated from high school or college (a fast-food coupon), got married or divorced (a cookbook).

Daytime Activities for All

1. **Excursions.** Visit a nearby scenic site, zoo, or other attraction. Take along a big picnic lunch.
2. **Hiking.** Set up a mini-camp in the shade for nonhikers. The hearty ones can enjoy their hike and then return for lemonade and cookies with the others.
3. **Revisiting the Old Neighborhood.** This works for a class reunion or for families who have lived in several houses in one town. Prepare in advance a list of addresses (including drive-bys at popular hang-outs) and travel in a bus or vans to visit the places. Sometimes the residences will no longer be there, but it is still interesting to see how the old neighborhood has changed. When this was done for a grade-school fiftieth reunion, the classmates were driven past each of their childhood homes—and this turned out to be the highlight of the reunion.
4. **Kids' Pageant.** Let teens help younger children present a pageant about the family, depicting the arrival of the family in this country, marriages, children, wartime service, career moves, and special events. It doesn't have to be entirely factual!
5. **Talent Show.** In the reunion invitation, ask guests to participate in a two-minute presentation of their talents, and to bring any instruments needed. Adults and kids can entertain one another by singing, dancing, reciting, playing an instrument, or telling a joke.
6. **Parades and Floats.** When many reunion participants live in one area, or when it is a college reunion, parades with floats are sometimes featured. For a small family reunion, youngsters can also have a parade with decorated bicycles, wagons, and strollers, plus music from harmonicas, drums, and kazoos.
7. **Sports.** Play softball, touch football, volleyball, soccer, or basketball with fairly chosen teams of all ages. If there's a pool, have water polo, races, and diving contests.

Games and Relays

1. **Tug-of-War.** With a long rope and a center line, and able-bodied family members lined up on two teams, see which side can pull the other over the line.
2. **Two Generation Three-Legged Race.** Make up teams of adults and kids for a relay to a marker and back. Use an old bedsheet torn into strips to tie one adult and one child's legs together.
3. **Gunny Sack Race.** Set up two teams, each with a gunny sack, and the oldest

family member as the marker around which the jumpers (inside the sack) must go. When they get back to the start line, the next team member takes over the bag and starts jumping.

4. **Miniature Golf Competition.** Make your own mini-golf course with sunken cans, boxes to shoot through, and other obstacles.

Just for Kids

Provide some activities just for young children: crafts, a clown to do face painting and simple magic tricks, hide-and-seek, and other suitable games. Have available various toys to keep the toddlers happy.

Music and Dance

1. **Sing-Along.** Late in the evening, let music take over. Sing songs everyone knows (or provide song sheets). Here are some multigenerational favorites: "Shine on Harvest Moon," "I've Been Working on the Railroad," "Yellow Submarine," "O What a Beautiful Morning," "Row Your Boat," "For Me and My Gal," "On the Sunny Side of the Street," "Raindrops Keep Fallin' on My Head," "I'm Forever Blowing Bubbles," "Seventy-six Trombones," "God Bless America," "Goodnight Ladies."

2. **Square Dancing.** This is a good three-generation activity. All you need are some records, directions for about four to six simple dances, and someone willing to teach them.

3. **Dancing.** Of course, having an orchestra or band would be nice, but a good DJ works well, too. Preview the selections and have a good mix of tunes for old and young. One of your group, or a professional teacher, can teach everyone a new dance. It's also fun to learn a dance from the family's heritage (a polka, schottische, hula, Mexican hat dance, or highland fling).

Other Evening Activities

1. **Family Quiz Show.** Divide the group into two teams. In advance, prepare a list of questions about the family history (specific questions about family members, jobs, number of kids, achievements, hometowns, and so forth) and see which team does best.

2. **Old Movies, Videos, or Slide Show.** Just twenty to thirty minutes of views from the past with a peppy commentary is all that's needed. More is boring.

3. **Storytelling Night.** This can take two forms: let the older family members tell stories from their past, or let everyone exchange names, interview that person, and then tell a story about him or her.

4. **Campfire.** While storytelling goes well around a campfire, so do roasting marshmallows and singing songs.

5. **Piñata Bashing.** Young kids especially like this activity, so have it first after the evening meal. Hang a candy-filled piñata and let blindfolded participants take turns hitting it with a stick or bat until it breaks open and there is a mad rush for the goodies.

Last Day of the Reunion

1. **Worship Service.** Although the group may be of different faiths, it is enjoyable for all to attend one church service together.
2. **Committee Recognition.** At the final meal, be sure to honor those who worked to put on the event.
3. **"Auld Lang Syne."** Join in a circle, holding hands or with hands around shoulders for the singing of this song. Here are the words adapted from the Robert Burns song meaning "old-times fondly remembered."

Auld Lang Syne

Verse 1:
Should auld acquaintance be forgot, And never brought to mind?
Should auld acquaintance be forgot, And days of auld lang syne?

Refrain:
For auld lang syne, my dear, For auld lang syne:
We'll take a cup of kindness yet, For auld lang syne.

Verse 2:
And here's a hand, my trusty friend, and give a hand of thine;
We'll take a cup of kindness yet, For auld lang syne.

Refrain

MAKE A TIME SCHEDULE

While the event may not stick to a preplanned schedule, it's still good to have one. Here's the time schedule for a Friday through Sunday twenty-fifth anniversary party we gave one August when we could use patios and other outside areas around our house. We invited twenty-five couples from around the country and from our hometown. About half stayed at a local inn. Local friends volunteered to help by providing pies, cakes, cookies, and flower arrangements.

Friday: Flowers, notes of greeting, schedule of events, and maps to our house delivered to the inn for out-of-town guests.

4:00-7:00 P.M.	Arrivals, name tags, appetizers at our home.
7:00	Buffet dinner featuring Mexican foods.
8:00	Storytelling: how we met each of the guests (in kindergarten, at a first job, at church, on a boat trip, and so forth).
9:00	Dessert and outline of the following day's activities (even though it was mailed to them, we went over it again).
Saturday:	Breakfast on their own.
Morning:	Sports and games. We had inquired in advance what sports each guest would be interested in and had arranged horseback riding, golf, and tennis for that morning, as well as bridge and other games at our home.
Noon:	Buffet lunch around the pool. The menu included five large sandwich loaves (made in advance, frozen, thawed that morning), served with chips, fruit, and cookies.
1:00 P.M.	Off to the Wild Animal Park (a world-renowned zoo for animals, complete with natural habitats, shows, and an hour monorail ride. A friend purchased the bus trip to the park and admission tickets as an anniversary gift. We had a busy three hours!)
5:30	Quiet time!
7:30	Dinner-dance at a small local club. It was a catered dinner with toasts, a twenty-fifth anniversary wedding cake, a silly musical play about our first twenty-five years (created by the guests), group and individual photos taken, and after my husband and I danced the "Anniversary Waltz," everyone danced until midnight.
Sunday:	Almost everyone slept late and breakfasted on their own.
10 A.M.	Worship service. Although our guests were of nine different denominations, they all went to church with us.
11 A.M.	Walking tour of our little town.
Noon:	Luau on the lawn. Hawaiian fruit salad, roast pork, sweet potatoes, banana bread, coconut cake.
1 P.M.	Special recognition of those who helped with the party, came the farthest, had the most children, were married the longest or shortest, or had won at their sports events.

144

1:30-3:30   Hawaiian music and dancing in the garden. "Aloha Oe" sung as the guests left for home.

LET'S DO IT AGAIN!

While the glow of a reunion lingers, and before the folks leave, get plans started for the next one. If possible, select the next date and take suggestions for the place. It's great if the next Coordinator volunteers!

Give participants a "What did you think?" comments form to fill out at the last event or to take home and send in. You'll get some well-deserved pats on the back but there's always room for improvement! Be open to all suggestions and don't be offended—you did your best!

Along with thanks to helpers, the Coordinator should send a photocopied or computer-produced follow-up letter to everyone. Some groups have a regular newsletter keeping them up-to-date during the intervening months or years. E-mail is a popular modern way to keep in touch, too.

WHERE TO GET HELP

You can be the "Little Red Hen" (and do it all yourself) but you can also get good tips from professional reunion planners. Here are some helpful sources of information:

1. Whether you're looking for a campsite or a ballroom, call the Chamber of Commerce or Tourist Bureau in the area you've chosen. Call the toll-free directory at 800-555-1212 to get specific phone numbers. A local travel agency can also give you helpful literature and costs.
2. Some helpful books: *Family Reunion Handbook* by Tom Ninkovich and Barbara Brown, *Recreational Ideas for Family Reunions* by Adrienne Anderson, *Reunions for Fun-Loving Families* by Nancy Bagley.
3. Learn how to make a family documentary from Gift of Heritage, P.O. Box 17233, Minneapolis, MN 55417, Phone 612-726-9432, Fax 612-727-2705.
4. Read *Reunions Magazine:* P.O. Box 17727, Milwaukee, WI 53211-0727, phone 414-263-4567, Fax 414-263-6331.

A SAMPLE TIMETABLE

While every event is different, here's a helpful timetable to guide you to a great reunion. Not all types of reunions will require all these duties.

Twelve months or more in advance:
❑ Discuss idea with others to determine their interest level.
❑ Send a first mailing, indicating date and possible location, and ask for names of others to invite.
❑ Set up a committee to aid the coordinator.
❑ Start a record-keeping systems.

Eleven months in advance:
❑ Select a location and reserve (hotel, campsite).
❑ Plan the theme and activities in general.

Ten months in advance:
❑ Create a mailing list from responses to the first mailing.
❑ Set up mailing labels for all mailings.

Nine months in advance:
❑ Send second mailing with definite information as to place, activities, and cost. Include reservation form for lodgings.

Eight months in advance:
❑ Select the guest of honor (if there is to be one).
❑ Choose a Master of Ceremonies.
❑ Decide on souvenirs such as T-shirts, mugs, and so on.

Seven months in advance:
❑ Set up the schedule for meals: at a hotel or restaurant, a catered potluck, for meals included at lodgings, and meals when attenders will be on their own.
❑ Reaffirm lodgings at hotels, in homes, and so on.

Six months in advance:
❑ Send the third mailing with many enticing details of activities.
❑ Include names of some of those coming, and make any special requests regarding talent, contributions of food, and so on.
❑ Hire any professionals such as photographer, caterer, or musicians.

Five months in advance:
❑ Obtain decorations, flags, streamers, balloons, and so on.
❑ Order printed items such as T-shirts.

Four months in advance:
❏ Organize volunteers and design definite tasks.
❏ Buy any special clothes you will need (including tux rental).
❏ Make a schedule of the way you hope the event will go.

Three months in advance:
❏ Send the fourth mailing with a complete time schedule of events.
❏ Make the family tree on large posterboard.
❏ Plan table linens, paper supplies, and needed utensils.

Two months in advance:
❏ Make and copy a directory of all attending with full information about each person, for giving out at the event.
❏ Prepare name tags.
❏ Prepare information for Master of Ceremonies.

Three to four weeks in advance:
❏ Send final reminder.
❏ Prepare a program of events including times and places.
❏ Reconfirm all reservations (entertainers, lodging, golf times).
❏ Prepare materials/supplies for all activities, photo displays, and games—also evaluation forms.
❏ Arrange with a responsible teen to oversee parking.

One to two weeks in advance:
❏ Prepare the foods that you are responsible for and can freeze.
❏ Decide on all clothing with family members.
❏ Go over the reunion schedule and pick up any loose ends.
❏ Get plenty of rest!

The day before:
❏ Be sure the house and yard are tidy.
❏ Make or buy ice for storing in ice chests or lined barrels.
❏ Set out needed chairs, tables, linens, and paper products.
❏ See to last minute food preparation, and defrost frozen foods.

Reunion Day:
❏ Place balloons and directional identification signs at site.
❏ Set up photo displays, decorations, and reception table.
❏ Have a great time!

❑ Give out evaluation forms asking guests what they liked best and least, opinions on lodging, food, activities, cost, location and (very important) their willingness to help for the next reunion.

After the Reunion:
❑ Write or phone thanks to all volunteers.
❑ Consider suggestions for improvement.
❑ Confer with next the Coordinator and transfer files.
❑ Send a follow-up newsletter

* * *

You can make a reunion a lot of work and no fun, or you can plan it slowly and carefully so that it is struggle-free. If you choose to thoughtfully plan ahead, you can enjoy every step of the way.

10

99 Ideas for Successful Parties

Party-givers who suggested ideas for this book gave many tips that are worth repeating. (You will find ideas on master-minding your party in chapter 2, and party themes with appropriate foods, decorations, activities, and gifts in the chapters that follow.) These additional tidbits will help make your party one of the bestever.

You'll find ideas for invitations, decor, good recipes, party themes, games, and prizes and favors.

PARTY INVITATIONS

1. **Not just 6 P.M.** Don't always think of parties as starting at conventional times. Have a Saturday morning brunch or a 9:00 P.M. movie-viewing party. One successful host entertains regularly from 4:00 to 7:00 P.M. on a weekend day. He says it allows plenty of time for daytime sports and guests still have the evening for a movie or time at home.

2. **Hard to find house?** If you think your party location will be difficult to locate in the dark (or even in the light), enclose a map in your invitation. Also state that there will be red (or some color) balloons on the nearest street sign and at the driveway. As a courtesy to the neighborhood, do remember to take down the signs and balloons after the party.

3. **Save money.** You don't have to put out big bucks for fancy invitations. A hand-written note, a postcard, or a computer-generated invitation works just as well and can save money and time. One party-giving couple bought a large supply of attractive bordered paper and matching envelopes. They use the paper in their computer/printer to give details of their parties.

4. **Keep a copy.** Invite yourself by keeping one copy of your invitation for your party notebook or scrapbook. This extra invitation also can come in handy when one person regrets and you need to send another.

5. **Mixing guests.** It's best when everyone attending a party knows at least one other person (besides you). New friendships can form at parties. So when making up your guest list, it's fun to mix guests from work, the gym, church, and the neighborhood.

6. **Whom do we owe?** Take time to make a list of your social friends (an easy computer job). Then note following each name the letter W (for we) and the date you entertained them. Example: Jacobson. W: 5/11/96. Do the same when they entertain you except use a T (for they). Example: Sherman. T: 6/16/96. In this way, you'll be able to quickly see whom you "owe" and how long it's been since you entertained them.

7. **Backward planning.** Let's say you're planning a Fourth of July bash. When should you send your invitations? For holiday times, send them early, using the following guide: The party week will be busy with getting the house in order and preparing foods. So, two weeks before, get certain elements of the meal ready and in the freezer. Three weeks in advance, plan any decor plus activities, games, favors or prizes. So, four weeks in advance is an ideal time to send out the invitations.

8. **What to wear.** When a host said that the jacuzzi would be the focus of a party, one guest couple arrived in swim suits—only to find that all the others were dressed for dinner, and had brought their swim suits to change into later. Be specific. Use words such as: casual, sporty, dressy, festive, formal.

9. **New acquaintances.** Keep enlarging your circle of friends. For a first get-together, make it just you and the new acquaintances for dessert or a movie. Then, if you seem to get along well, include them in a larger party the next time. Keep alert to new neighbors and new faces at your activities—these are sources for expanding your friendships.

THE PARTY ATMOSPHERE

10. **Don't forget outside!** Here's a list of outside things to check before guests arrive: Is the house number visible? Are the driveway and yard clear of toys/rubbish barrels? Are the obvious garden chores finished? Is the car in the garage, not taking up a parking space in front of the house? Are the garage doors closed? Assuming that guests have already showered, are the sprinklers along the sidewalk turned off? Is the garden hose neatly coiled off the walkway? Are the porch and sidewalks swept? And, if it's winter, are the walk and steps free from snow and ice? Are the outside lights working?

11. **Don't forget the inside!** On party day, walk in your front door and see what a guest will see. Is the entry uncluttered? Are the sofa cushions and throw pillows plumped? Do you have adequate seating? Are the level surfaces in the party area free from clutter and personal items? Is the kitchen tidy enough, considering you're cooking? Is the bathroom clean and stocked with soap, towels, and tissue? Is there adequate lighting and/or candles?

12. **Music hath charms.** Well, some music does. For background music at a party, avoid radio stations with long commercials and commentary. Better to select recorded music that is nonvocal. Try to find music that ties-in to your theme—lively music for active parties, semi-classical music for card and game parties.

13. **No flowers?** You can make an impressive table arrangement without a single posie. Set the table with white linens. Down the center of the table, use long mirrors (called table runners, and inexpensive to buy at a craft or glass shop). Then place crystal candleholders of staggered heights on the mirrors. Use two twenty-four inch white candles near the center, and smaller ones toward each end. Cut tree branches twelve to eighteen inches in length and spray them white. Arrange these among the candles. You can also adapt this idea for other parties by using colored candles and spraying the branches a compatible color to go with your linens.

14. **Cozy nest.** Plan a party around the fireplace, using low chairs or cushions so that everyone is close to the fire. Cook cocktail franks as an appetizer and marshmallows for an after-dinner treat. To make the room extra cozy, turn off most all the lights and close the draperies.

15. **A crafty idea.** Even if you aren't a Martha Stewart clone, a trip to your local craft store will supply you with many useful, inexpensive and easy ideas for decorations, table settings, activities, and prizes. If you haven't yet discovered the wonders of a glue gun, ask to see one. Even the most fumbling fingers can work wonders with this inexpensive tool.

16. **Party in the park.** Your taxes have paid for your local parks, so use them! Some will require a permit that entitles you to a certain location. A covered area is ideal for eating, the grassy area for games, the play equipment for the kids. Balloons indicate your party area and colorful ribbons can claim your tables.

17. **Magical world.** Although your backyard may not be a botanical garden by daylight, it can look grand for an evening patio party. Dig out those tiny Christmas lights and string them in trees and large shrubs for a fairyland look. And don't forget to spray in advance for bugs, or burn several citron candles.

18. **Three roses.** So you don't have a flower garden? Buy just three roses and ask for some free greens to go with them. Use them like this to brighten your party: Place one in a slender vase and put it in the powder room. Float the second one in a low glass dish or brandy snifter on the coffee table where guests will gather. The third one goes in the center of the dining or buffet table, surrounded by greenery that you've sprinkled with glitter.

THE PARTY TABLE

19. **Words of wisdom.** A couple who gives parties once a month says they don't hesitate to repeat a successful menu as long as the guest list is different. It gets easier and faster as they perfect the preparations. However, their aim is to offer an

enjoyable and stimulating evening, not just fabulous food. And if the meal doesn't turn out to be great, that's O.K., because they know that the guests are going to eat again the next day!

20. **So you hate to cook?** If you still want to have a dinner party, here's a solution that's more unique than a potluck, cheaper than a caterer, and can also benefit a good cause. It's to ask church ladies to prepare the dinner. Many churches have groups of talented women who are happy to provide dinner—even serving and clean-up if you wish—for a reasonable cost.

21. **Presentation is priceless.** The way food *looks* on the buffet table or on individual plates is highly important. Decorate with a twist of citrus, a small bunch of grapes, or a small rinsed flower or leaf-cluster. Be sure that edges of serving dishes and plates are free from food spills or splashes. On a buffet table, allow room at the front so that a guest can place her plate there while serving herself a hard-to-dish-up item. Place the entrée first and the side dishes next, with gravies, sauces, butter, and so forth at the end. If tables aren't set up with cutlery and napkins, these should be the last items on the buffet. It helps if you can have a separate area for beverages.

22. **Light up a meal.** Who says that candles are only for birthday cakes? You can make meals festive by using small candles on many desserts: pie, pudding, ice cream balls. One host even placed a lighted candle in a rounded scoop of mashed potatoes!

23. **Red is the color.** Own red tablecloths large enough to fit all your tables. You can make them inexpensively from plain red yardage featured at Christmas, but you'll find that the red color is also great for Valentine's Day, Fourth of July, and birthday parties.

24. **Finger bowls are back.** Nowadays we're eating more finger foods and with pizza, corn-on-the-cob, chicken legs, and barbecued ribs, hands can get really sticky. Although finger bowls were formerly served at the end of the main course of a formal dinner, many party-givers are now putting a small finger bowl at each place, right next to the drinking glass. A lemon slice in the water adds a nice touch and finger-dipping saves on messy-stained napkins.

25. **Terry cloth linens.** Colorful terry cloth hand towels make good table linens for patio parties or kids parties. And for kid wash-ups, provide a roll or box of folded paper towels in the bathroom. (Unless it's an elegant affair, avoid the printed paper hand towels that can cost up to twenty-five cents each.) Consider that terry cloth hand towels don't require ironing, are inexpensive to buy at a linen discount store, or can be made out of your unneeded towels. They look festive rolled and piled in a basket on the bathroom counter.

26. **Forget dinner.** It seems that when dining, many folks prefer less food and less calories, so you needn't build your party around a huge feast. Consider entertaining at other eating times: breakfast, brunch, lunch, or dessert. One hostess never has guests sit down at the dinner table. She just prepares many interesting yet nutritious appetizers—enough for a meal—and lets guests choose how much or how little to eat. Some call this "grazing."

27. **Theme foods for a potluck.** Your friends may enjoy bringing part of a well-planned potluck meal. For a Swedish smorgasbord I once served, I even offered simple recipes to those non-Scandinavians making the very special dishes. The table had labels such as "Stephanie's meat balls," "Clarence's limpa bread," "Leslie's rice pudding." It made for great conversation—and compliments—and the cooks learned some new recipes.

28. **Take a break.** Often a lovingly prepared and spectacular dessert isn't appreciated right on top of a huge meal. It is a nice tradition to break after dinner for conversation or games and activities. Then, near the close of the party, reassemble at the table for dessert and the awarding of the prizes. It makes a classy closing touch.

29. **Save trees and money.** A runaway paper napkin can result in fancy footwork or floor-crawling to retrieve it. But a cloth napkin is far more efficient and stays put. Watch for linen sales and buy a quantity, choosing only the permanent press type. In the long run, they're money-saving, environmentally correct as far as trees and landfills are concerned, and they're easy-care for you. Plus, they look more luxurious on the table.

30. **Napkin folding.** Borrow a library book and copy two or three attractive ways to fold napkins. Keep this information in with your recipes or entertaining file so you can find it before your parties. Distinctive napkin folding makes even the plainest napkin look elegant and many husbands enjoy doing the intricate folding.

31. **Bibs are no shame.** For an adult party with sloppy food (such as spaghetti or lobster), put a paper bib at each place (purchase the bibs at a party store). Guests will get into the spirit of fun while tying them on. And for truly messy fingers, you may want to tuck a paper napkin inside the cloth one. For kid parties with messy foods, let children use marking pens to decorate their paper bibs.

FAVORITE RECIPES

32. **Best-ever appetizer: Cheese Crispies**

> ½ pound (2 sticks) margarine
> ½ pound sharp cheddar cheese
> 2 cups flour
> ¼ teaspoon cayenne pepper
> ¼ teaspoon salt
> ⅛ teaspoon curry powder
> 2 cups rice crispies cereal

Cream margarine and cheese together in mixer. Add flour with pepper, salt, and curry. By hand, add rice crispies. Form into balls and flatten with a fork. Bake in 350 degree oven for eighteen to twenty minutes until very lightly browned. Serve when cool.

33. **Best-ever main dish: Nutty Salmon**

    2 tablespoons Dijon mustard
    2 tablespoons melted margarine
    2 tablespoons honey
    ½ cup bread crumbs
    1 tablespoon dried parsley flakes
    1 tablespoon dried onion flakes
    ¼ cup pecans, chopped fine
    4 five-ounce salmon fillets (fresh or frozen/thawed)
    Salt and pepper for seasoning
    Lemon wedges

Mix together first three ingredients and set aside. Mix together next four ingredients and set aside. Season fillets with salt and pepper and place on greased baking pan. Spread honey-margarine-mustard mixture on each fillet. Top with bread crumb-parsley-onion-nut topping, pressing topping firmly into place. Bake in a 450 degree oven about fifteen minutes (depending on thickness of fillet). When it flakes, it is done. Serve with lemon wedges. Four servings.

34. **Best-ever salad: Elegant Eggplant**

    1 medium eggplant, peeled and sliced 1/2 inch thick
    Salt
    4 Italian tomatoes, coarsely chopped
    1 cup finely chopped fresh parsley
    1 bunch finely chopped green onions (entire onion)
    Romaine or red leaf lettuce

Salt eggplant slices and place on paper towels in a glass pie plate or other dish suitable for the microwave. Cover tightly and microwave on high for three minutes. Rinse and thoroughly dry eggplant and chop fine. Mix with tomatoes, parsley, and onions.

Prepare dressing of one-fourth cup olive oil, two tablespoons cider vinegar, one-fourth cup lemon juice, three crushed garlic cloves, and one tablespoon sugar. Mix well and toss with salad. Season with pepper or salt as needed. Serve on lettuce leaves.

35. **Best-ever potatoes: Magic Mashed Potatoes**

Who says you can't make wonderful mashed potatoes in advance!

    5 pounds baking potatoes, peeled, cut into cubes, cooked until soft
    1 8-ounce package of cream cheese at room temperature
    1 cup of sour cream at room temperature
    1 teaspoon garlic salt
    ½ teaspoon pepper
    Salt to taste
    ¼ pound butter or margarine

Drain cooked potatoes and mash in a large electric mixer bowl. When thoroughly mashed and lump free, gradually add the cream cheese and sour cream and mix thoroughly. Add seasonings to taste. Spread mixture in a large flat casserole and dot with butter. At this point, casserole can be refrigerated for 48 hours, frozen, or baked. Before baking, bring to room temperature and bake at 400 degrees for forty-five minutes to an hour—until heated through and slightly browned. Let sit five minutes before serving.

36. Best-ever bread: Onion Bread
This recipe is for an automatic bread maker. Place ingredients into bread maker in this order:

> 1 package yeast
> 3¼ cups better-for-bread flour
> ¼ teaspoon baking soda
> 4 tablespoons sugar
> ½ cup grated Parmesan cheese
> 1 egg
> 1 envelope of onion soup mix

Slightly warm the following ingredients and add:

> ½ cup cottage cheese
> 1 cup sour cream
> 2 tablespoons butter
> ¼ cup water

Setting should be for white bread, middle range of doneness.

37. Best-ever dessert: Blue and White Torte

> Crust:
> 1½ cups graham cracker crumbs
> 3 tablespoons sugar
> ¼ cup (½ stick) plus 2 tablespoons melted butter

Mix together and press into nine-inch pan that has a removable rim. Bake at 350 degrees for about twenty minutes.

> Topping:
> ¼ cup water
> ¾ cup sugar
> 3 tablespoons cornstarch
> 2 cups blueberries (fresh or frozen)

In a saucepan, mix sugar and cornstarch, then stir in water and blueberries. Cook and stir over high heat until mixture boils and thickens. Let cool.

Filling:
1 cup white chocolate chips
1 8-ounce package cream cheese
¼ cup sour cream

Reserve one tablespoon of chips. Melt remaining ones in microwave or over boiling water and stir until smooth. When slightly cool, add cream cheese and sour cream and blend. Spread evenly on crust and top with blueberry topping. Refrigerate until cold. Before serving, place reserved chips in a blender to finely chop, then sprinkle in the center of the torte.

PARTY LOGISTICS

38. **Throw-away cameras.** These are a wonderful idea for weddings, and this idea is adaptable for other large parties. Place on each dining table a small disposable camera with just twelve exposures. Tell guests to take pictures of everyone at the table and anything else they like at the event. Collect the cameras at the end of the party and have the pictures developed. These candids are often more interesting than the professional ones, and also assure you that each guest is in at least one picture.

39. **Balancing act.** Don't rush your party by having one event immediately after another. Allow time for conversation and fellowship. A good party balances the time spent on eating, talking, and playing.

40. **Traysful of fun.** Establish a tray or shallow box for each game or activity at your party. Mentally go through the event and place on the tray everything you'll need for a specific game or activity: paper, pencils, magazines, blindfold, prizes, rubbish bag, and so forth. Keep the trays in a cupboard or closet until you're ready for that activity.

41. **All in the family.** Parties that include both parents and children can be among the best, but when you're having an all-adult event, you can still include *your* youngsters for part of the party. Let the children indicate where cars can be parked, take coats and jackets, and serve appetizers. Let older kids (who can be trusted with the china and want to earn some extra cash) cleanup after dinner.

42. **Which fork?** Some rules of etiquette have changed in the recent decade, but good manners are still in vogue. Buy a new etiquette book and you'll find many great party ideas, as well as how to write invitations, introduce strangers, and where the dessert spoon goes.

43. **Start with a bang, end with a bang.** Don't condone late arrivals at your parties. Always be ready with the appetizers and start with a mixer about fifteen minutes after the announced time. When the party is over, don't sit around until you or a guest falls asleep. Announce: "This will be our grand finale" or "This is the final round." Don't wait for "the fat lady to sing," although one hostess does start a chorus of "Goodnight, Ladies, Goodnight Fellas" as a not-too-subtle hint that the party is over.

44. **"What can I do to help?"** When a guest says those magic words, have a ready answer. Here are some suggestions: Pick up empty glasses, napkins, food from appetizer time. Or, rinse and stack dinner plates. Or, pour the coffee. Or, put extra food into the refrigerator for later packaging. Such "helps" let you keep the party moving and free up your time to be with guests. And, some guests enjoy helping and will feel more a part of the family.

45. **Thirty minutes before.** No host likes to start a party with the kitchen sailing in dirty dishes and messy counters. Spending ten minutes before the party to bring order out of chaos makes the cleanup afterwards much easier. Also, place a bowl of sudsy water in the sink so that used cutlery can be placed in it before the food becomes permanently attached to the silverware.

46. **The boy next door.** Or the girl next door. Teens are often looking for extra spending money, so hire a responsible young person to help at your party. Have him arrive in advance of the guests so you can tell him his exact duties. Be specific, and if there are many assignments, write down the work to be done.

47. **Safe going home.** If you will be serving alcoholic beverages at your party—or if you suspect that young guests have brought liquor into your party—you are morally and legally responsible for your guests' safety as they go home. Some will willingly subscribe to the "designated driver" system. Others may say "I'm fine." But be insistent for their well-being and your liability. Call a cab, call a relative, create a carpool, or drive the guests home yourself.

48. **Party perfect.** In the week before a child's party, discuss certain manners: welcoming guests, thanking for gifts, how to handle duplicate gifts or gifts not liked, eating the foods to be served, blowing out candles (without spitting), and saying good-bye to each guest. On the day following the party, help a child to send thank-you notes or make thank-you phone calls.

49. **Spreading out the guests.** For a large party, you don't want people clustered at the front door, obstructing incoming guests. So, place the punch bowl or other liquid refreshments as far from the door as possible so that guests will move in that direction. Then, place the appetizers in various locations: on the patio, in the family room, on the hall table. This moves guests around and helps them meet more people.

50. **Be prepared.** Look over the guest list in advance and consider what problems might arise: argumentative relatives, shy (or pushy) friends, spaghetti sauce on the carpet, a late arrival, an early departure, a person with food dislikes, a TV sports special that may try to intrude on your plans, a long silence in the dinner table conversation. Think over how you would handle each situation, what you would say, what you would do, how you could adjust. You're much more likely to be a relaxed host if you're armed with these contingency plans.

51. **When you've been the guest.** When you've been entertained, remember to thank the host/hostess. On the day of their party, when you have the invitation with their address on it, make out an envelope to the host, and stamp it, too. Leave it on your desk as a reminder the next day to write the note and send it off.

52. **Who writes the note?** Good manners are both feminine and masculine. One husband we know has always been the one to thank for parties. The day after an event, he either pens a note or calls the host and hostess and tells them how much their party was appreciated.

53. **After the party.** Ask yourself how successful it was: food, beverages, music, activities, decor. Was it worth the time and cost? Record your ideas in your party log (see chapter 2).

PARTY THEMES

54. **Start at the door.** If your party has a theme—babies, birthday, or bingo—introduce the theme right at your front door. Putting up a drawing of a big baby face with one tooth, a huge birthday cake, or a big bingo card will underscore the theme. And, when all the guests have arrived, take down your drawing and tape it on the powder room door.

55. **First day of spring.** It's growing time! One couple living in a mild climate celebrates with a garden party—the kind where the guests get to plant pots and plots. The hosts have the plants, potting material, and tools ready for action. Guests divide into teams for an hour of horticulture. Vegetable seeds are planted, patio flowers are potted, shrubs are pruned. Then the workers are rewarded with a steak dinner, followed by thank-you gifts of new trowels, plant foods, and seeds.

56. **First day of summer.** This picnic in the park works well for about four families. It begins with food prepacked at home in baskets for two—one adult and one child (not related to each other). The menu includes chicken or ribs, potato and fruit salads, king-size cookies and pudding. The pairings result in interesting conversations! Then it's time for contests: water balloon tossing, egg relay, croquet. As these games wind down, two adults have laid a trail for the treasure hunt that will lead everyone from trees and swings to barbeque grills and fences. Back at the gathering area there are warm-weather prizes for everyone (suntan lotion, sand pails, jazzy sunglasses, soft drink holders, caps).

57. **First day of autumn.** Rent a cabin for a day (day use and the fact that it is the off season will make the price very reasonable). Take along binoculars, a bag of old bread, an iron, pinking scissors, and wax paper cut into sixteen inch sections (two pieces for each guest). Also the food and dishes for a hearty lunch: lasagna, garlic bread, tossed salad, apple pie. Invite friends and families to spend the day at your

"private lodge." When everyone has arrived, go for a walk to collect colorful autumn leaves. Back at the lodge, let the group put the old bread in places where the birds and other animals might find it. Then, while lunch is warming, hand out the wax paper pieces so that each person can arrange his leaves in an attractive design on one piece of paper. Then, show how to add the second piece of wax paper on top of the arrangement and, with a moderately hot iron, press the two pieces until they are fused. Each guest then cuts the edges with the pinking shears to make a place mat for lunch. After lunch, use the binoculars to see the distant views and close-up birds. Also, check to see who is eating the bread. Before leaving for home, divide into twosomes and play hide-and-seek in the crisp fall air.

58. **First day of winter.** Go where there's snow for a party with several families. Pack thermos bottles with hot chocolate and coffee plus doughnuts for a morning snack, hearty meat and cheese sandwiches to serve with baked apples for lunch, and brownies for the going-home snack. Take along sleds, toboggans, garbage can lids— whatever will slide down the hill. When the free-play fun begins to wear off, start contests: fastest sledding time from start line to finish line, slowest time from start to finish, most people on one sled, and so forth. Divide into teams for a snowball fight, have a snowman-building competition, find undisturbed snow and make snow angels. Write your names in the snow before leaving.

59. **Square dancing.** Convert your garage to the square-dance floor. Put chairs around the sides, place colorful sheets over stuff you don't want visible, use recorded music, and have a big table of beverages and snacks for the breaks between dances.

60. **Breakfast with the ground hog.** The long cold winter often needs a humorous spark, so consider a party on Ground Hog Day. According to legend, the ground hog, or woodchuck, awakens from a deep sleep each year on February 2. When he sticks his head up out of his hole and looks around, he also is predicting the weather ahead! If it is sunny and he sees his shadow, he's frightened back into his hole for six weeks of wintry weather. But if the day is cloudy and he can't see his shadow, he happily stays above ground, indicating that spring will soon come.

While there's no scientific data to back up these predictions, it's still an occasion to party. Invite friends to stop on their way to work or school for your "Breakfast with the Ground Hog" party. Serve juice, waffles with hot syrup and mugs of cocoa or coffee. Go outside to check for sun or clouds so you'll know whether there will be spring or more winter. Take a picture of the group before sending them on their way.

61. **April 15 tax party.** If misery loves company, why not gather friends for an April 15 tax party, asking them to come in their poorest clothes and to bring a good idea on how to save money or increase income. Serve "Poor Man's Dinner": baked beans with frankfurters, crusty bread, cole slaw, coffee and plain doughnuts. Use aluminum pie pans as plates, newspaper for tablecloths, clean rags for napkins, old used candles as the centerpieces. After eating, start the sharing of good fiscal ideas.

62. **Housewarming.** Do it Japanese style. Surprise your friends even before they move in by asking to see the house one evening—and then surprise them with a group bearing housewarming gifts. Encourage everyone to leave shoes at the front

door. Since most towns now have a Japanese deli, buy a variety of finger foods for your unique supper. Sit on mats on the floor for food, drink, and gift opening.

63. **Sports night.** Invite guests to come dressed for their favorite sport. Be sure to take a group picture since there will be quite a variety of clothing. Plan activities that tie-in with sports: putting golf balls, badminton, volleyball, Ping Pong, relays, and so on. For weird fun, try bowling with an eggplant and empty quart milk cartons.

64. **Kite flying.** A daytime party for families (or just kids or grown-up kids-at-heart) can be built around kites. Have plenty of inexpensive kite kits, string, and tails on hand, and begin the party with assembly time. Let each person letter her name on her kite with a marking pen. Then go out to fly the kites at a windy spot such as the beach or an open field, away from power lines. Have lots of prizes for first kite in the air, first to crash, last to crash, first to tangle, highest, and so forth.

65. **The bus party.** A rolling party can be fun. Some cities still have trolley cars to rent, but most common is a midsize bus (you'll find these companies listed in the classified telephone directory). You can choose a destination or just stay aboard and view the sights. Provide box drinks and food easily eaten with the fingers. Bring song sheets. Play team games such as Scattagories or Third of a Ghost pitting the left versus the right side of the bus.

66. **Veterans' party.** One group of people who don't get many parties are veterans—the men and women who have faithfully fought for our country. Consider planning a party at a veterans hospital or retirement home. Call the activities director and find out what foods and entertainment would be appropriate. Activities can include the playing of box games, cards, and puzzles, and some vets just enjoy good conversation. Along with food gifts, consider supplying stationery and stamps, audio recordings, and magazines. If possible, include youngsters in the preparations and events since many vets don't have much contact with young people. While this party may not be the most festive you've ever given, it very well may be one of the most appreciated.

67. **What's my decade?** Plan a party around the ten decades of this century. Ask guests to come dressed from one of the decades, and when everyone is present, line up in chronological order from the 1900s to the present. Find old records or tapes and try dances from the past. Try foods and drinks from earlier years such as root beer floats (1910s), poor man's stew (1930s), Spam sandwiches (1940s), Asian foods (1970s), and so forth.

68. **Martin Luther King Day.** On this day, parades, speeches, and parties should not be limited to African Americans. Dr. King's messages were ones of equality and love for all people. Become acquainted with someone of another race through your youngster's school, your church or club, and your work place—sites where you will find people whose company you will enjoy. Make the get-together informal and low key, perhaps just dessert, or sledding followed by hot chocolate. One family reports that a very successful party started when they entertained a family of a different race that they had met at church. The next year, these two families each invited another family, making four families—of different ethnic roots. And, the next year they did

the same. They reported that they soon had "the United Nations of Cincinnati" for their annual event.

69. **Moving out party.** Who likes the giant chore of packing up dishes and books? We were invited to a moving party and asked to bring many sturdy boxes. First, we were fed hamburgers with seven different toppings. Then, the group was divided into teams and assigned areas to pack: kitchen cupboards, bookshelves, toys, linens, even the fine china. Breakables were carefully wrapped and the box sides were padded, then each finished box was clearly labeled. We were invited to put a message in each box we completed—something to cheer the family when it came time to unpack all those boxes.

70. **Hanukkah: Feast of Light.** It is a genuinely enriching experience to share a Hanukkah event. This Jewish holiday is called the Feast of Lights or Feast of Dedication. The word *Hanukkah* can be written *hannuka* or *Chanukah* and means feast. Occurring in December and lasting eight days, it celebrates the Jews' defeat of the Syrians about one hundred and sixty-five years before Jesus' time. The festivities were held in the Jerusalem temple which the people were cleansing of desecrating Syrian idols. They could only find one cruse of undefiled oil to use for their holy lamps, but miraculously, the lamps burned for eight days. The leader, Judas Maccabaeus, proclaimed the festival which is still held today. Along with wonderful foods, small gifts are exchanged and charitable contributions are made, but more important is the lighting of the eight ceremonial candles of the candelabrum—one each day. This is a very special and holy party and if you give one or are invited to observe this event, you will find it a memorable experience.

71. **Beach castles.** An ordinary beach party can be extra fun if you have a castle-building contest. Bring trowels, pails, and various sizes and shapes of plastic molds. Divide into teams of both adults and kids, about three or four to a team, and let them get to work. Have awards for the best castles, houses, swimming pools, golf courses, and so forth. Top the day off with a fish-fry, sand volleyball, and sand croquet.

PARTY GAMES AND ACTIVITIES

72. **Conversation starter.** On the inside or back of the place cards at the dining table, write an unusual secret word such as bodacious, eclectic, cyclical, outlandish, peripatetic, sluggish, monumental. Each person must try to work his word into the conversation without being caught. At theme parties, such as a baby shower, you can use related words: burp, diaper, crawl, rattle, and so forth.

73. **Gloop.** Many kid games can be played with this substance that is both slimy and gooey, yet lots of fun for an *outdoor* game. In a large pail, mix one part water to four parts cornstarch. (Add food coloring to the water for an interesting effect.) Let youngsters stir it to a consistency like thin sour cream, adding more water or cornstarch for just the right consistency. (Prepare it just before using, as it hardens.) Divide the group into two relay teams. Place the pail on the start line and two bowls about twenty-five feet away. A player from each team picks up a handful of gloop and

then runs from the pail to his team's bowl, depositing the gloop there. He runs back to the start line and the next team member does the same thing. First team to fill the bowl wins. Kids should wear old clothes, the grass will need to be hosed down at the end, but everyone will have a grand time.

74. **No dance floor?** Teens (and many parents) love to dance and if you can foresee several years of dancing, go together with other neighborhood parents to buy a dance floor. All you need is large paneling pieces that can be stored along a garage wall or in the rafters between parties. Dance floor wax and some elbow grease will make the floor shine.

And the mirrored ball? Of course you could buy an expensive one, but you can make one inexpensively. Go to a glass and mirror company and ask to have all the broken mirror pieces they have. Wearing gloves, carefully break the broken parts into small pieces and then very firmly glue them to an old soccer or volleyball. Industrial strength glue will hold the pieces in place. Hang it on very sturdy fish line over your dance floor and position a spotlight and fan on it, so that it twirls and sparkles.

75. **What can this be?** Collect a number of mystery objects that are easily identified when seen, yet hard to identify when handled with rubber gloves while blindfolded: a spray can, drapery hook, a child's book, a soda cracker, powder puff, a toothpaste tube, a tube of glue, coaster, syringe—as many objects as there are guests. Keep all the objects hidden. Then, blindfold and glove one person at a time and hand her one of the objects. She is to tell three ways to use the item. Some ways will be correct, but many of the uses will be wildly inappropriate and funny.

76. **Church bells ring.** Many churches have bell choruses—groups who practice bell ringing and give performances—especially at the holiday season. For a donation or nominal fee they will come to your Christmas party and put on a show, including explaining the bells and the history of chiming. You can even sing some carols along with them.

77. **Racing arachnids.** Make two *sets* of spider legs by stuffing newspapers into old tights sewn together (you'll need four pairs of tights, two for each set). Using a belt, show how to strap these onto the players stomachs. Divide into two teams for arachnid racing from a start line to a goal about forty feet away. The first player straps on the extra four legs and then gets in the crab position (back to the floor with hands, legs, and the four extra spider legs touching the floor) and creeps toward the finish line and back. Then, the extra four legs are belted onto the next racer and the game continues until one team wins.

78. **The secret videographer.** Rather than lining up people and making them say "cheese" to a thirty-five millimeter camera, let a person with some videotaping talent be in charge of capturing unique or funny moments at your party. These could include kitchen preparations, arrivals, feet under the dining table, someone yawning, games, and so forth. Before the guests go home, play back these highlights of the party.

79. **Rock around the block.** Following a large feast, suggest a quick walk around the neighborhood. Guests will return to your home relaxed and ready for the activities you've planned.

80. **A letter of recommendation.** Each guest puts her name on the top of a large piece of lined paper. These are collected and redistributed. Now each person is to write an anonymous but sincere, factual, or humorous letter of recommendation for the name received, a letter pointing out the persons strong-points and weaknesses—*all in jest.* After about 10 minutes, collect the papers once more and return them to the original people who now must read aloud what has been written about them. Finally, they must try to guess who wrote the letter.

81. **Wreath-making.** At a pre-Christmas party for youngsters or adults, have the supplies needed to make wreaths: plenty of greens, the wire to tie them into a circle, plus decorations: stars, tiny ornaments, ribbon, fake fruits, glitter and spray snow. Divide into teams, each team making two wreaths. Provide work tables and tools, plus a rubbish can for easy cleanup. Award prizes for the best wreath and let guests take them home or donate them to charitable groups.

82. **Shy guest?** Many party-goers are intimidated by games—at least at first. If you have a hesitant guest, give him a special assignment such as being the scorekeeper, handing out equipment, keeping time, or assisting you in serving the snacks. Perhaps he'll later join in after seeing everyone having such a good time.

83. **Portrait painters.** For a party with ten or more guests, provide lots of colored marking pens, plain paper, and thick magazines. Place the names of each guest on separate slips of paper and let each person choose one. Sitting in a circle, guests go to work on their easels (the magazines) and make a portrait of that person without obviously staring at him. When everyone has finished, the artist holds up his work and the group tries to guess who it is.

84. **Teen favorite.** One teen came back from camp and introduced the whipped cream fight to his friends. All you need is a backyard, a whistle, a string circle about fifteen feet across, guests in swim suits or old clothes, and several large cans of whipped cream (buy the cheapest spray cans available). Divide the group into teams who sit on opposite sides of the circle. One nonplayer has a whistle that he blows about every twenty seconds. When the whistle blows, a player from each team enters the ring and fires whipped cream at her opponent. When the whistle blows again, these players hand the can to another team member and the fight continues. There are no winners or losers, just a hosing off of all the players at the end.

85. **TV or not TV?** Guests can stay home and watch television. They come to your house for something different. Let guests know in advance if TV is going to be part of your activities, and make certain that it is something special: a classic that you have rented just for the occasion, a film that ties in with your theme, a once-a-year sports event, or your own recording of an exceptionally funny show.

86. **No trifle.** This activity has an edible result! One party-giver lets guests make the dessert from England—and although it is called trifle, it's no trifle. It is made early in the party, but served at the very end. In advance, buy or make a small pound cake and an angel food cake. Cut these into big bite-size pieces and place in bowls. On a kitchen counter place many ingredients such as vanilla custard, chocolate sauce, strawberry jam, fresh or canned peaches, orange segments, white chocolate chips,

marshmallow cream, and whipped cream. Guests gather around the counter, each by one of the ingredients. First, some of each cake is placed in the bottom of a large glass bowl which is then passed around as some of the other ingredients are added, then more cake, then more ingredients, more cake, and so forth. During the assembling, use a spatula to lightly press the layers together. Top with the last of the whipped cream and refrigerate for several hours. Using a large spoon, serve in dessert bowls. There will be calls for seconds!

PARTY FAVORS AND GIFTS

87. **Best ten favors/prizes for adults:** Homemade foods such as jams and flavored vinegars, purchased foods such as fudge sauce or can of nuts, small plants, interesting magazines, pretty paper napkins or hand towels, coffee mugs, paperback mysteries, Post-it notes in a holder, candles, fireplace logs.

88. **Best ten favors/prizes for teens and preteens:** Audiotapes, hand-crafted jewelry, unique caps, thermal soft drink holders, movie passes, interesting magazines, jazzy pens, sunglasses, belts, mystery games.

89. **Best ten favors/prizes for preschoolers:** Stickers, plastic dinosaurs, play jewelry, crowns, marking pens, books, play foods and dishes, toy construction or farm equipment, fantastic bubble stuff, sing-along tapes.

90. **For someone who has everything.** A great gift for the hard-to-buy-for person is an American flag. Flag prices are very reasonable and you can choose one for outdoors, or for use on a car aerial, or on a stand for displaying on a desk.

91. **Hostess gifts.** When someone comes in the front door and hands you flowers, candy, wine, or whatever, thank the giver and place the gift on a table where it can be seen. However, you are not obliged to serve food or drink items unless it fits your plan. Always keep a vase handy so you can quickly put flowers in water and place them in the party room. Slip a Post-it note next to a gift that doesn't have a card and write on it the giver's name—that way you'll know who brought what when the party is over.

92. **What's popular?** Before a child's party, visit a toy store together. You will learn two things: First, what things interest her and might make good gifts. And second, what small items fascinate her and would be good party favors.

93. **Gifts to the honoree.** Showers and birthday parties mean gift-opening—which can be either fun or boring for the guests. Observers will enjoy watching and talking, but don't let this part of the celebration creep along too slowly. The honoree should read the cards and name the giver in a clear voice. The host (or parent) should help the honoree by having one person keep a list of what's received, another to take charge of the wrappings and ribbons, and another to place the card with the gift and pass it around for all to view (since every guest wants to see every gift).

94. **Use your noodle.** Kids can make jewelry and Indian headbands from uncooked noodles threaded with yarn. Color the noodles this easy way: Mix one-half cup of rubbing alcohol with a little yellow food coloring and immerse noodles, then dry on

newspaper covered with wax paper. Add blue food color (to make the mixture green) and repeat the process. Then start with red food color. Next mix in blue food color to make a purple mixture. Now you have four colors of noodles. For easy threading, put a small piece of tape on the end of the yarn.

95. **A gift that lasts a year.** As a gift to one special person, gather twelve snapshots which have meaning in her life: her children, other close relatives, home, a special car, vacation site, pets, and so forth. A favorite choice is to specialize in pictures of her grandchildren. Instant-print shops will turn these into a personalized calendar for the coming year with a different large photo for each month. (The original photos will be returned to you.)

96. **Make it official.** If the party is in someone's honor, get a certificate from a local official. Mayors, city council members, fire and police chiefs are often happy to give recognition to long-time residents and worthy citizens. For birthdays eighty and over or anniversaries fifty and over, you can write for a greeting card from the President of the United States. Write: Greetings Office, The White House, Washington, D. C. 20500.

97. **What happened that day?** You can surprise a couple on their anniversary or a person on his birthday with a copy of an actual newspaper published on the day of their wedding or birthday. It's a great souvenir of your party and everyone present will want to read it. The papers cost about twenty dollars and they are readily available in catalogs.

98. **King-sized YOU.** In many mail-order catalogs and also at some instant-print shops, you can supply a photo of a person or a beloved pet and have it made into a giant poster. It makes a great gift for a birthday or retirement. Put it up on the wall of the party room for all to see before sending it home with the honoree.

99. **Candle power.** After Christmas, buy up—at bargain prices—all kinds and colors of candles. Some you can save for the next Christmas, others make wonderful game prizes or hostess gifts during the year.

* * *

Now you have the tools, the good ideas, and most of all, the incentive to be a creative party giver. Keep this book as your guide for years to come and start a file of your own successes. You'll find that party-giving is a great way to bring friends and family together!

THE PARTY-GIVER'S CREED

*I entertain because I enjoy being with old and new friends.

*I don't feel that food and drink must be the focus of a party.

*I do my best to make everyone feel at home at my parties.

*I try to reciprocate by entertaining those who entertain me.

*I know that entertaining is not a competition but a gift.

*I include my family in planning and carrying out social events.

*I let my guests help me with my celebrations.

*I plan ahead so that I'm not frantic and exhausted when

　entertaining.

*I try new activities and foods without hesitation.

*I accept some failures as part of the process.

*I keep a record of my entertaining.

*I enjoy going to my own party.

*I know that entertaining is an extension of my love for others.

Index

Adult parties, 23-41, 156-158
April Fool's Day, 98

Christmas, 109-113

Decorations, 150-51
    Artist Party, 51
    Bridal Shower, 117
    Halloween Party, 105
    Old MacDonald's Party, 71
    Olympics Party, 63
    Party Table, 151-53
    Safari Party, 60
    Snowball Party, 49
    South Seas Islands Party, 29
    Thanksgiving table, 107
    TV Party, 69

Easter, 98-99

Food/Refreshments, 152-53
    Animal Party, 54
    Anniversary Party, 119
    Artist Party, 52
    Clown Party, 67
    Crazy cones and cupcakes, 75
    Culinary-judging Party, 127-30
    Dress-up Tea Party, 47
    Flower Power Party, 100
    for grade-schoolers, 74-76
    for teens, 80, 90
    for young children, 56
    Old Macdonald's Party, 72
    Olympics Party, 65
    Peek-a-Boo Sandwich, 75
    Reunions, 137
    Safari Party, 62
    South Sea Island Party, 30
    Sweet Sixteen Party, 85
    TV Party, 70
Father's Day, 102-103
Flag Day, 102
Fourth of July, 103

Games and activities. *See* also Ice
    Breakers
    A Funny Thing Happened . . . ,
      120
    A Shelf of Cans, 35
    A Taste Test, 36
    Adorable Babies, 84
    Advice Game, 119
    Anniversary Mixer, 119
    Art Hunt, 52
    Artist's Fence, 52
    "Ballooney" Sandwich, 67
    Beanbags, 56
    Bell Ringers, 162
    Bible Charades, 125
    Birthday Suit, 84
    Blindfold Portraits, 51
    Bubble Blowers, 87
    Buried Treasure, 45
    Carol Game, 110

Caroling, 109
Categories, 85
Cherry Twist, 125
Chicken Coop, 71
Circle of Light, 109
Clown I. D. Cards, 66
Coach's Nightmare, 90
Conversation Starter, 33, 161
Cookie Decorating, 56
Corn-eating Race, 107
Cracker Whistling, 125
Crazy Clown Catches, 67
Creeping Through the Jungle,
    61
Dress-up the Doll, 48
Dunce, 85
Face-painting, 66
Find the North Pole, 50
Finding a Partner, 32
Flower Arranging, 100
Flowery Game, 118
Follow the Animal, 53
Football Guessing Game, 96
For neighborhood activities, 123
Front and Back, 53
Giant's game, 74
Gloop, 161
Good Sports, 64
Grateful Chain, 107
Hat Hunt, 47
Hat-making, 66
Hayride, 71
Hidden Books of the Bible, 126
Hidden Geography, 86
Hide and Seek, 48
High-Wire Act, 66
Hot, Warm, Cold, 50
How Many Beans?, 71
Human Conveyor Belt, 74
Island Mysteries, 29
"I'm Going on Safari" 61
"I Went to the Mall," 89
Jungle Treasure Hunt, 61
Kitchen Hide-and-Seek, 127
Larger than Life, 119
Laughing Cowboy, 72
Letter of Recommendation, 163
License Plates, 37
Love Song Charades, 97
Making a TV Show, 69
Midnight Walk, 114
Musical Games, 28
Musical Balloons, 56
Mystery Objects, 162
Mystery Sacks, 113
Name Five, 74
"Name That Tune," 105
No More Doublespeak!, 124
Olympics Obstacle Course, 64
Outrageous Adjectives, 87
Pancake Race, 99

Penny Hunt, 55
Pentathlon Games, 25
Photo Contest, 108
Picture Lotto, 50
Pin the. . ., 56
Piñata Bashing, 108
Pirate Bottle Knockers, 45
Pirate Fishing, 45
Pirate Maps, 46
Pool Party game, 73
Pool Obstacle Course, 84
Portrait Painters, 163
Potato Relay Race, 63
Practical Pachyderms, 114
Pumpkin Relay Race, 106
Pumpkin-carving Contest, 106
Pushin' Peanuts, 66
Racing Arachnids, 162
Resolutions, 96, 113
Reunion Activities, 141-43
Robbery, 89
Sailor's Toes, 84
Scavenger Hunt, 73, 88
School Art, 85
Secret Videographer, 162
Sink or Swim, 46
Sinking Ship, 83
Snapping game, 88
Square Dancing, 72,
"Stranded," 29
String Maze, 88
String 'Em Up, 46
Sunrise Celebration, 104
Super Marksmanship, 64
Super Sleuths, 90
Taste Test, 36
Tasting Game, 119
Tell the Truth, 33
Ten-yard Dash, 63
The Lion's Tail, 61
Toasts and Roasts, 117
Trike Relay, 85
Tunnel Race, 55, 105
Twisted Titles, 111-12
Typhoon, 83
Vegetable Animals, 74
Walk the Plank, 46
Water Targets, 123
Weight Guessing, 125
What's On the Tray?, 74
Whipped Cream Fight, 163
Who's That Cute Baby?, 120
Window Painting, 52
Wreath-making, 163

Grade-school parties, 59-76
Grandparent's Day, 104-105

Halloween, 105-106
Hanukkah, 161
Holiday parties, 95-114

Ice Breakers, 32, 45, 47, 49, 51, 53, 60, 63, 66, 69, 71
Invitations, 16, 25, 27, 29, 45, 47, 49, 51, 53, 60, 63, 65, 69, 97, 99, 100, 102, 149-50

Labor Day, 104
Large Parties, 19

Martin Luther King Jr. Day, 160
May Day, 100
Memorial Day, 101
Mother's Day, 100-101
Music and dance
    at Reunions, 142-43
    for teens, 79, 162
    "I'm a Song" Dinner Party, 27
    Karaoke, 80, 98
    Love Song Charades, 97
    Musical Games, 28
    "Name That Tune," 105

New Year's Day/Eve, 95-96, 113

Party-Giver's Creed, 166
Planning Your Party, 11-21
Preschool Parties, 43-57
Prizes and Gifts, 50
    Anniversary Party, 117
    Bon Voyage Party, 121
    Candles, 165
    Clown Diploma, 68
    for adults, 164
    for preschoolers, 164
    for preteens and teens, 164
    from officials, 165
    Honoree gifts, 164
    Hostess gifts, 164
    Noodle Necklaces, 164
    Old MacDonald's Party, 72
    Olympics Party, 65
    Posters, 165
    Reunions, 139
    Safari Party, 62
    Special Newspapers, 165
    Take-home Purses, 48
    TV Party, 70

Recipes
    Blue and White Torte, 155
    Bunny Cake, 54
    Cheese Crispies, 153
    Chicken Ole', 39
    Chocolate Eclair Cake, 91
    Chocolate Truffles, 97
    Clown Cones, 67
    Critter Crunch, 92
    "Eat Your Peas" Salad, 92
    Elegant Eggplant, 154
    Exotic Fruit Salad, 129
    Fruit Slush, 91
    Hearty Soup, 38

Heavenly Ham Salad, 127
Magic Mashed Potatoes, 154
Minestra, 81
No-leftovers Appetizer, 38
Nutty Salmon, 154
Onion Bread, 155
Orange-Potato Salad, 130
Peppy Pea Salad, 128
Savory Pasta Salad, 129
Tempura, 27
Texas Sheet Cake, 75
Tiger Cake, 62
Trifle, 163
Two-week Cabbage Salad, 39
Volcano Cake, 40
Reunions, 131
    basic planning, 132
    excursions, 141
    food, 137
    games and relays, 141
    mailings, 136
    music and dance, 142
    opening event activities, 140
    photography, 138
    professional help, 145
    selection of date, 133
    selection of place, 133
    setting the theme, 134
    souvenirs, 139
    time schedule, 143-48
    who pays what, 136
    who to invite, 135

Special occasion parties, 115-30
St. Patrick's Day, 97-98

Teen parties, 77-93
Thanksgiving, 106
Themes for parties
    Academy Award Party, 122
    Animal Party, 53
    Antonio, the Super Chef, 81
    April 15 Tax Party, 159
    Artist Party, 51
    Baby Shower, 119
    Backwards Progressive, 87
    Barbeque Get-Together, 115
    Beach Party, 161
    Bon Voyage Party, 121
    Bridal Shower, 117
    Bus Party, 160
    Casserole Shower, 120
    Church Friends Party, 125
    Circus Party, 54
    Clown College Party, 65
    Cookie Party, 111
    Couch Potato Party, 87
    Culinary-judging Party, 127
    Dress-up Party, 47
    Equestrian Party, 31

Fairy Tale Party, 55
Field Trip Parties, 73
First Day of Season Parties, 158-59
Flower Power Party, 31
Gifts for a King Party, 11
Graduation Celebrations, 116
Ground Hog Day Party, 159
Heavenly Party, 30
Hobo Party, 73
Housewarming Party, 159
"I'm a Song" Dinner Party, 27
Investment Club Party, 30
Karaoke Party, 80
Kite Flying Party, 160
Mall Party, 73
Microwave Magic Party, 31
Moving Out Party, 161
Mystery Party, 31
Mystery Sacks Party, 113
Neighborhood Party, 123
New Resident Party, 116
Old MacDonald's Party, 70
Olympics Party, 62
Pancake Party, 80
Penguin Party, 73
Pentathlon Party, 25
Pep Party, 83
Photographic Progressive Dinner Party, 31
Pirate Party, 44
Poetry Party, 31
Politically Correct Party, 122
Puzzle Party, 32
Retirement Party, 121
Safari Party, 60
Snowball Party, 49
Something's Wrong Party, 31
South Seas Islands Party, 29
Sports Party, 55
Square Dancing Party, 159
Stuff Santa Party, 112
Sweet Sixteen Party, 84
Swimming Pool Party, 83
"Teacher Let the Monkeys Out" Party, 85
Tempura Party, 26
Time Capsule Party, 24
Train Party, 55
TV Party, 69
Veteran's Party, 160
Wake-up Party, 72
What's My Decade Party, 160
Wild and Wet Party, 83
Wild West Shoot-out Party, 72
Wizard of Oz Party, 55
Women's Welcome, 115

Valentine's Day, 96-97